Anonymous

Warming and Ventilation for Public Buildings, Schools, Halls,

Stores & Dwellings

with a description of the Hess

Anonymous

Warming and Ventilation for Public Buildings, Schools, Halls, Stores & Dwellings
with a description of the Hess

ISBN/EAN: 9783337090654

Printed in Europe, USA, Canada, Australia, Japan

Cover: Foto ©Andreas Hilbeck / pixelio.de

More available books at **www.hansebooks.com**

Geo H. Hess Co

·THE·HESS·

WARM AIR

HEATING and SYSTEM

VENTILATING

ENGINEERS

CHICAGO

Warming and Ventilation

—FOR—

PUBLIC BUILDINGS, SCHOOLS,

Halls, Stores, Dwellings, Etc., Etc.,

With a Description of the

· HESS ·

"Pure Air" Furnaces,

Heaters, Cooking Stoves,

Ovens, Fire-Places; &c.

MANUFACTURED BY

THE HESS STOVE WORKS,

GEO. H. HESS CO'Y, PROPRIETORS.

Main Office & Salesroom

286 Franklin Street.

Foundry and Works:
286 to 302 Franklin Street,
206 to 218 VanBuren Street

CHICAGO.

Hess Portable Steel Furnaces.

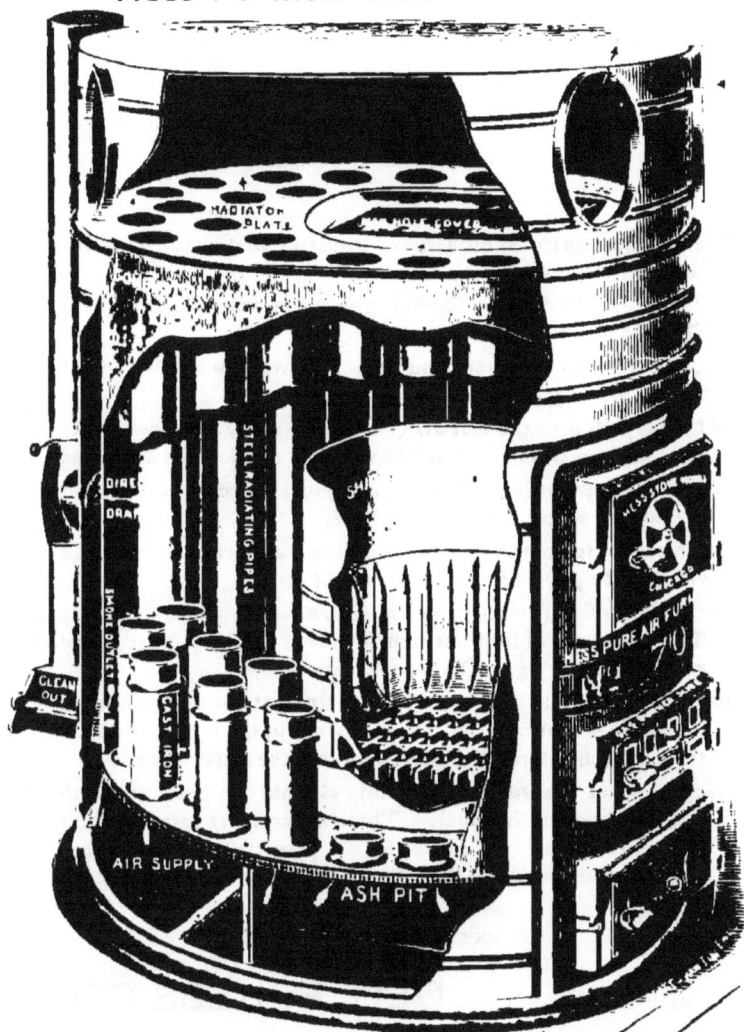

NOS 51-2, 61-2, 71-2, 50, 60 AND 70 OVAL

This style furnace is made in ten sizes from 5 to 7 feet high. Hard Coal, Soft Coal or Wood. Burns Soft Coal without black smoke.

"The indispensable conditions attached to a good furnace are a good chimney draft and a large combustion chamber. The ordinary furnace is very faulty. When the products of Combustion are flying off to the chimney at the speed of 30 feet a second, it must be clear that 50 per cent of the heat is lost.—

How to Choose Heating Apparatus.

TO GET ESTIMATE OF COST OF FURNACE WORK

Send Plan of house drawn to a scale, showing size of rooms to be heated, location of doors, chimneys, etc , height of ceiling, including basement.

Give points of compass

1. The purchase price should *never* govern—that you pay but *once*—the fuel you buy yearly.
2. *The Greatest Radiating Surface* gives the *most heat* for the fuel used. There is no other index of power.
3. Select a size *larger* than you *need*. It will save fuel and care, and is better than a guarantee.
4. Get what will give the *best air* (steam and many furnaces fail to give it). This air you inhale. Your health and comfort are concerned.
5. Select an apparatus that you can govern according to the weather. Steam and many furnaces fail here.
6. Get something simple in construction—and easy to manage—unless you like to pay bills and be annoyed.
7. For claims of superiority, *get a reason*, and use your *own* judgment. This is an age of improvement. Men are no longer satisfied with goods past the age. The world moves.
8. Be certain that the men you buy of understand the principles of heating and ventilation. Because they are in the business does not prove they have mastered the science or had the experience.
9. Keep in mind the *fact* that in this climate we must use artificial heat *seven months* in the year. There is no more important question in the construction of your house. A powerful and economical heating apparatus is worth all it costs. *The best will prove the cheapest in the end.*

Respectfully,

GEO. H. HESS CO.,
CHICAGO.

HESS PURE AIR TUBULAR STEEL FURNACE

Nos. 1 A, 5, 6 and 7.

Hard Coal, Soft Coal, Coke and Wood.

PRICE LIST AUGUST 1887.

(ALL OTHER LISTS VOID.)

HEATERS AND HEATING STOVES.

No.	Width of Case, inch.	Depth, Inches.	Height, Inches.	No. of Air Tubes.	Inside Size of Firepot	In Inches.	Cubic Inches of Combustion Chamber	Square In. of Heating Surface.	Cubic Feet Capable of Heating.	Amount of hard Coal Required per Average Winter, other fuel in Proportion.	Price.
1	13			2	8×5	5,150	2,211	1,200 to 1,500	½ to 1 ton nut.	18 00
2	14				10×6	8,394	3,776	2,000 to 2,500	1 to 1½ ton nut.	20 00
3	16				12½×8	11,340	5,476	3,000 to 4,000	1½ to 2 nut or range.	45 00
4	19	20			14×9	17,211	8,314	9,000 to 12,000	2 to 4 range.	50 00
5	25		70		15×11	25,542	10,045	10,000 to 18,000	2 to 4 range.	75 00
6	34		78	12	17×10½	24,307	13,646	25,000 to 25,000	4 to 5 coarse range.	90 00
7	42		78	18	20×12½	14,931	17,487	25,000 to 35,000	1 to 6 small egg.	115 00
			78		25½×13	50,315	19,520	40,000 to 50,000	6 to 9 large egg.	140 00

FURNACE HEATERS.

No.					Firepot		Cubic	Square	Cubic Feet	Coal	Price
4	30		70	9	15×11	25,542	10,105	12,000 to 20,000	2 to 4 range.	85 00
			73	13	17×10½	30,934	13,660	20,000 to 30,000	4 to 5 coarse range.	100 00
			74	15	20×12½	48,960	16,560	25,000 to 40,000	4 to 6 small egg.	135 00
	44		74	17	22½×13	50,349	19,425	30,000 to 70,000	6 to 9 large egg.	170 00
			74	17	17×11½	52,072	22,610	50,000 to 80,000	4 to 6 coarse range.	145 00
	52		73	17	20×16½	76,902	28,170	60,000 to 55,000	5 to 7 small egg.	185 00
20			74	19	22½×17½	101,004	30,640	60,000 to 100,000	8 to 12 large egg.	225 00

FURNACES.

No.											Price
4	30		77	9	15×11	25,542	10,205	9,000 to 12,000	2 to 4 range.	85 00
5	33		74	12	17×10½	27,394	13,170	12,000 to 18,000	3 to 5 coarse range	100 00
6	40		74	13	20×12½	42,174	16,367	20,000 to 25,000	4 to 6 small egg.	135 00
7	42		80	15	22½×13	80,046	19,185	30,000 to 65,000	6 to 9 large egg	170 00
8	55		80	17	15×23×9	35,692	16,050	12,000 to 16,000	3 to 5 coarse range	125 00
9	42		80	17	17×27×11	50,841	16,690	20,000 to 25,000	4 to 6 small egg	160 00
10	73		80	19	17×30×11	8c,991	20,105	90,000 to 55,000	6 to 9 large egg.	200 00
11	52		74	17	15×34×14	80,022	21,051	25,000 to 40,000	4 to 6 coarse range	145 00
12	65		74	19	18×37×14	64,576	24,400	30,000 to 40,000	5 to 7 small egg.	185 00
13	70		74	19	21×30×14	101,562	25,155	40,000 to 50,000	8 to 12 large egg.	225 00
14	70		74	24	24×38×16	101,094	25,340	60,000 to 90,000	13 to 19 large egg.	450 00
15	70	108	74	36	28×47×16	144,854	35,676	90,000 to 140,000	16 to 24 "	840 00
100	70	118	74	53	28×48×16	230,400	56,476	130,000 to 180,000	30 to 40 "	730 00
110	70	181	74	65	28×60×16	307,300	70,070	160,000 to 180,000	35 to 40 "	850 00
100	70	181	74	84	28×72×16	384,100	90,100	200,000 to 240,000	50 to 30 "	1,000 00

Vertical Wheel Registers and Ventilators. Japanned: Black or White.

SIZE OF OPENING	REGISTER.	WITHOUT VALVES.	REGISTER FACE.	FLOOR BORDER.
4×13			30 85	
6×8			0 85	
8×10	2 50	1 75	0 85	1 40
8×12	2 80	2 00	1 00	1 50
9×12	3 50		1 25	1 55
10×12	3 80	2 75	1 50	1 55
10×14	4 25		1 85	1 80
12×15	5 00	3 00	2 1	1 90
14×18	8 75		3 50	8 15
16×24			5 00	4 65
20×20	15 00		10 85	5 00
27×27		ASTRA HEAVY FOR STONE ETC.		7 50
30×30				8 00
80		HEAVY SQUARE REGISTER FACE ENDS		9 00
36			11 50	14 00

Hot Air Equalizing Registers, made only by us. Japan and Bronze Finish.

18×18 .... $16.00   Opening 14×14 Requires 14-inch pipe.
18×21 ...... 20.00   " 14×18 " 16 " "
21×21 .... 25.00   " 18×18 " 18 " "
21×30 .... 34.00 ..... " 16×24 " 20 " "

The above sizes of Registers we manufacture and carry in stock. They are heavy and strong, equal in all respects to the best makes. All other sizes will be furnished to order.

WRITE FOR DISCOUNTS.   SEE NEXT PAGE.

HOW TO ORDER HEATERS OR FURNACES.

Select a size *larger* rather than *smaller* than you require. Slow combustion is economical. Forcing the fire wastes the fuel and burns up the castings. Bear in mind, also, that *we heat the whole space* to the same degree, and if the stove is too small, no spot will be warm enough to suit you. Any of our goods will hold fire from 15 to 24 hours, with hard coal and proper management.

The amounts of fuel used is gathered from reports of customers. When it exceeds the above average to any great extent, it is the result of careless firing or loss of heat. Furnaces will be reduced in height without charge. In ordering state the kind of fuel used ; also height of basement, if furnace is wanted.

We keep a large corps of skilled furnace workers, and are at all times prepared to supply the necessary tin pipes, registers, etc. We would be pleased to make estimates on any work, and will guarantee results. Will make special rates in quantities or for introduction.

READ "HOW TO CHOOSE HEATING APPARATUS" ON FIRST PAGE.

N. B.—All prices given cover the cost of delivery and setting up in Chicago, or on board cars, and includes furnace cases, except for Nos. 80, 90, 100, 110, and 120, for which we furnish castings only for outer cases, whether brick-set or portable. Nos. 1, 2, 3 and 4 are mounted ready to use. All larger sizes are too large and heavy, and are shipped in "knock down."

Our terms are cash on delivery, but if the money is sent *with the order, or when the goods are ready for delivery*, a discount of 5 per cent. is allowed.

PRICE LIST OF COOK STOVES, ETC.

No. 9 Duplex Economy Steel Range,—for all fuels, weight 325 lbs			$45 00
No. 9 " " Oven Triple Case, asbestos lined, " 32 "			6 00
No. 9 " Water Back for tanks			5 00
No. 9 " Water Back and Reservoir			6 00
No. 9 Hess Range, "Economy," for hard and soft coal and wood, weight 110 lbs			$14 00
No. 9 Oven, 16x20 inch, triple case, weight 32 lbs			6 00
			$20 00
Hot Water Reservoir attached to Economy			$ 4 00
No. 8 Summer Stove, "Double Quick," weight 61 lbs			7 00
No. 9 Summer Stove "Double Quick," " 71 "			9 00
Double Quick Oven, right hand only, " 20 "			5 00
Set Drip Pans, to fit oven			50
Covered Sauce Pans, 2 qt., 20c ; 3 qt., 30c ; 4 qt.			40
Aunt Mary's Double Wire Broiler and Cover			85
3 3½, 5 and 6 inch Elbows, refined iron, each			25
Stove Pipe 5 and 6 inch, refined iron, per joint			20
Taper Joint, to fit 5 or 6 inch pipe			35

In ordering Cook Stoves, *state the kind of fuel to be used*, whether hard or soft coal or wood ; also whether the oven door is desired *on* the right side or the left—as you face the stove. If pipe is ordered, give distance from floor to centre of the hole in the wall with a diagram of pipe, and the pipe will come to you all fitted and easy to set up.

N. B.—Discount of 5 per cent. when cash accompanies the order.

When you order, read the description of Stove etc., carefully to prevent mistakes.

HILE this Catalogue is sent out as a business matter, we desire to convince its readers that we have not misstated or overdrawn anything. We have made a great advance in the science of burning fuel, of heating, and of ventilation. We have tried to make it simple and easily understood, so each person may be able to judge for himself whether these things be true. Our theories are reduced to practice, and to convince new customers of that fact, we append the testimonials of several prominent men, who investigated the subject before purchasing, and to whom we now refer, believing their direct personal testimony will have more value than whole pages of printed testimonials from obscure parties.

THE HESS STOVES, FURNACES, &c.

HE Stoves, Furnaces, Bake Ovens, Open Fireplaces, etc., made at the Hess Stove Works, under various patents, are departures from ordinary methods of construction. They have been thoroughly tried and have "stood the test." And it is admitted that they *stand ahead* of all others for *healthfulness, power* and *economy.* They are made on scientific and common sense principles.

The opinion prevails that one must burn so much fuel for so much heat, and that a stove or furnace should have flues through which the smoke may pass and give off what heat they will before the smoke gets into the chimney. *As the hot smoke travels through the flue at the rate of thirty feet per second,* it is plain that the loss is enormous.

When a fire is made out of doors, the air above the centre of the fire rises rapidly, and carries the smoke with it, but so soon as the smoke separates from the heat, it has no power *in itself* to continue to ascend, but either floats with the wind or settles back to the ground.

Now if we make a fire in a stove large enough to hold a considerable amount of the products of combustion, as they leave the fire, we will observe the same process in the stove that we saw in the open air; that is, the hottest portions will pass quickly to the highest point, until stopped by the top of the stove, *and they will be held there,* the cooler portion falling to the bottom. The air therein, finding its level as readily as water, and lying in strata, is always hottest at the top, and each

8

stratum below is cooler than its neighbor above. Aware of this unchanging law, we put our smoke pipe or escape *at the bottom*, thereby exhausting, or drawing away, *only* the coolest portions of the smoke and the heavy non-combustible gases. By no natural power can the heated air above pass down through the cooler strata to the bottom, but each stratum will float, in suspension, in its proper place, being *at all times* under perfect control, and in the power of its master, man, who can make it do his bidding. It may seem wonderful that the heat attacks the top of the stove with such immense force in its frantic efforts to get higher. This leads one to doubt whether modern stoves can have much power *when the heat produced in them meets no resistance, but, on the contrary, is assisted by wide-open flues in flying away at the rate of thirty feet in a second of time.*

By having a volume of heated air above and surrounding the fire-pot, the combustion goes on slowly, perfectly and automatically. The fire thus checks itself, and as we use it and draw away the heat, making the chamber cooler, it will burn more freely.

In this age of improvement, why continue to buy stoves made in the old way, when you know that *more than one-half* the heat goes up the chimney? There is no sense or science in using a stove or furnace or open grate that burns up TWO tons of coal, if you can find a way to make ONE ton do the same work. The *Hess Stoves, &c., now in use are saving from 40,000 to 50,000 tons of coal per annum.*

PURE AIR.

IT is a fact that nearly all Dwellings, School Rooms and Public Meeting Rooms HAVE NO PROVISION for ventilation: no outlet for the foul air, and all inlets for fresh air are closed in cold weather. To make matters worse, the air comes in CONTACT WITH VERY HOT CAST IRON. Carbonic oxide is also sent out through the pores of the iron and the cracks of the stove. Carbonic acid gas is also sent out from the lungs. Thus do these two poisonous gases mingle in the atmosphere to be taken into the system, PRODUCING HEADACHE, STUPOR, SENSE OF OPPRESSION, NERVOUSNESS, SICKNESS, FEVER AND CONSUMPTION. Consumption thrives upon foul air. It can be PREVENTED and HAS BEEN CURED by PURE AIR ALONE. To the sick or weak it is better than food or medicine. There are about 72 pulsations of the heart every minute, and at each pulsation five ounces of blood are passed through the lungs—an amount equal to more than 120 barrels per day, to be aerated. It is, then of the UTMOST IMPORTANCE that the air should not be deprived of its oxygen or poisoned, or even tainted, but that it should be pure and life-giving.

This is especially true of SCHOOL ROOMS, where numbers of growing children spend many hours every day. Trustees should not be satisfied with mere HEAT. Usually stoves are kept very hot. Those nearest are too warm, while those at a distance are freezing. All are in danger of taking cold, which would not be with pure air and an even temperature.

Why will you continue to use a heater that poisons the air you breathe, gives you headache, weakens your lungs or makes you sick? You know that air passing over red-hot iron is not fit to inhale.

"The exact nature of the change that highly heated metal produces upon air is not very well understood. It cannot be said to burn it, in the proper sense of the word, but it gives it a peculiar odor, which is both unpleasant and unwholesome. This is thought to arise in some measure, it least, from the hot iron burning the particles of dust that light on it, which particles consist of organic matter, such as wool, wood, etc."—*Chambers' Encyclopedia.*

WHY IS THE AIR PURE FROM THE HESS HEATERS?

Because while the air which surrounds the fire-pots of ordinary stoves, etc., is taken into the lungs, in the Hess Stoves and Furnaces it goes into the fuel and is used to promote combustion; *it helps to burn the smoke ; it unites with* and *consumes the gases.* YOU CANNOT INHALE IT. Everything is so perfectly consumed that you *can see nothing leave the chimney,* and the residue is—dust of ashes.

The fresh air is carried in upright wrought-iron or steel tubes through the combustion chamber *behind and away from direct contact with the fire,* and thus is heated by indirect radiation. This brings air into the room of a *pure, pleasant, summer temperature,* health-giving to young and old. Children and plants will thrive, the sick get relief and comfort, the lungs breathe freely. Bad feelings and headaches, so common with cast iron stoves and furnaces, are no longer suffered, but instead, an *invigorating* atmosphere gives tone to the system.

HOW DO WE SAVE FUEL?

BY using an unusually large combustion chamber and reservoir* to hold the products of combustion, and give them time to part with their heat. Heat does not go through even thin iron instantly, and much longer time is required for very thick cast iron. And we save

---

*The No. 3 fire-pot holds *but one peck of coal* within a combustion chamber containing 11,540 *cubic inches.* It has a case 31 inches in diameter, 40 inches high, with *six* upright air tubes running through it, affording a radiating surface of 5,476 *square inches.* It is capable of heating comfortably *six thousand cubic feet* of space all winter, requiring but *one and a half* to *two tons of coal,* under ordinary conditions, in this climate.

fuel by having our smoke outlet at the *base* of the combustion chamber. and also by having *no smoke flues* of any kind *within* the heater to lead away the smoke. As the products of combustion leave the fire very hot, they go at once to the highest part of the reservoir, and as fast as they lose their heat through this great radiating surface, they become *heavy* and *settle to the bottom*, when they enter the smoke flue, along with the *heavy, non-combustible* and *poisonous gases.* The heated portions will rise in the reservoir, but *cannot* fall, except as they become cool and are crowded down by the greater heat constantly rising above them. Do not confound our smoke outlet at the base with the common return flue. *We burn all the fuel, the gases and solids. We save the heat we make. Our smoke pipes are cool.* We have *no smoke flues or channels within* the reservoir to conduct away the heat or to become clogged with soot and ashes.

When smoke passes through a flue it deposits soot and ashes, which adhere to the inside of the flue in a thick coat, constantly accumulating. This reduces the heating surface, and being a non-conductor of heat and growing thicker, *prevents radiation.* When smoke enters a flue, combustion ceases for want of oxygen; when dampness gets into the smoke flues the iron is eaten up by rust.

Reverse this. Pass *air* through the flues and hot smoke outside. What do we find ? The soot is consumed, and the *flues* are kept clean, the heating surface always remains the same, and every inch of it is available; the flues *are preserved.* These are some of the features which give the Hess heaters their great power to heat and their durability.

CONSTRUCTION OF FURNACES.

CAST iron is used throughout except for the case and air tubes, which are of *wrought steel plate,* to radiate rapidly. These being upright, there can be no accumulation of soot and ashes to eat into the steel. In consequence, they are *very durable and remain proof against rust for years.* The superiority of wrought iron pipes over cast iron in a furnace is well known. Cast iron will expand and open the joints, and will crack and emit gas, and then trouble begins: as they radiate more slowly, they require more fuel. We are satisfied that our combination makes the *most durable furnace.* Let our cast iron fire-pot crack ever so badly, no gas can escape, but must *go directly into the com-*

bustion chamber and be consumed. As the air is not injured, no water pan is needed, though furnished if wanted free of charge.

In the first Hess Furnaces, made in 1878, as in all new constructions, the workmanship was somewhat crude. But when a defect was found, it was removed; where an improvement was possible, it was added, until now, after years of changes, the first furnace and the present make are similar only in principle.

The tubes and radiating surface are *annealed steel plate,* made expressly for our use. At the base of each tube is a *cast iron section,* ten to twelve inches high, to keep the tube out of the accumulation of soot and ashes, and to prevent rust of the tubes. The fire-pot is replaced by a heavier one, made in sections, and is a *perfect smoke and gas-burning fire-pot* for hard coal—the only one ever made—being perforated with 16 to 48 vertical air cells leading into the body of the coal and corrugated on the inside to keep the coal away from the metal, making the most durable pot in use.

As the air passes up through these air cells it becomes superheated, thus preparing it for immediate combustion, and by its entrance at so many points thoroughly mingles with the gases as they are evolved, and when ignited, fills the furnace with flame. It is claimed by some that there is as much latent heat in the volatile gases and smoke which ordinarily escape as in the solid parts of fuel; therefore, if we burn these lighter portions, it is reasonable to believe that we are gaining much increased heat. This pot is made in heavy sections, and so dovetailed with socket joints that it cannot fail to operate properly, and will not come apart even if broken. It can be used in all our stoves and furnaces heretofore made.

OUR NEW SOFT COAL FIRE POT:

AFTER experimenting several years, we now have ready a new soft coal pot for all sizes of furnaces and stoves. Its construction is such that the gases and smoke are almost entirely consumed. This is accomplished by the introduction of numerous jets of superheated air into the fire in such a manner as to mingle with the products of combustion, before they leave the fire, *forming a cyclone movement.* A large amount of flame is produced, developing intense heat, thus doing away with the chief objection to soft coal, viz.: *black smoke* and *soot.*

The fact that *the gases and the black smoke are converted into flame and heat,* gives our goods such an advantage over other makes, as to make up their greater cost in a very short time. These pots are simple, easily regulated; are made of cast iron; are durable and inexpensive to repair. They will fit nearly all sizes of furnaces made by us since 1882.

IN all the Furnaces and Stoves we use a grate with space between the fingers, increasing in width from the center and having *no outer rim.* This allows a ready clearance, for no stone or clinker can possibly become lodged. It readily shakes or dumps. It has proved—on account of this feature and its simplicity—to be of more real service than any other grate we have used.

The fire-pot and grate are brought to the front, and a door is placed above the grate to facilitate the removal of ashes, etc., and consequently the furnaces are easier to care for. The fire is controlled by a slide in the ash door, a check wheel in the feed door, a damper in the smoke pipe—all in sight. Nothing more is needed. *Every joint* is furnished with a *cemented collar*, making leakage of gas *impossible.* A heavy cast iron front is substituted for the small door frames of the old style, adding to the appearance of the goods and insuring *gas-tight doors.*

With these improvements, the Hess Furnace stands without an equal for *power, durability, quality of heat* and *freedom from gas.* The price is as low as for inferior goods, and when other goods are offered at a less price, the difference would be quickly made up by their greater economy of fuel.

These furnaces are made in *fourteen* different sizes and for all kinds of fuel, have separate fire-pots for hard coal, soft coal and wood. Three of the sizes are *but five feet high,* made expressly for low basements. The other sizes, averaging seven feet, will be furnished *any height* desired.

We have knowledge of all complaints since our first Furnace, and to this date—after eight years—the proportion of failures to heat have been but 25 to 30 in a thousand. We increased the sizes in three-fourths of that number. The remaining 6 or 8 have been substituted by other systems. In this small number the failures have been traced to imperfect setting or some fault in the premises beyond our control. THIS IS A GRAND RECORD. We guarantee our goods to do just what we claim, and if the conditions are complied with, and a furnace of proper size is properly set, with a good chimney draft, we are always willing to furnish one of a larger size if the first one proves inadequate. We would even guarantee the amount of fuel if we could control the fire-man. But the average amounts reported by our customers we consider reliable.

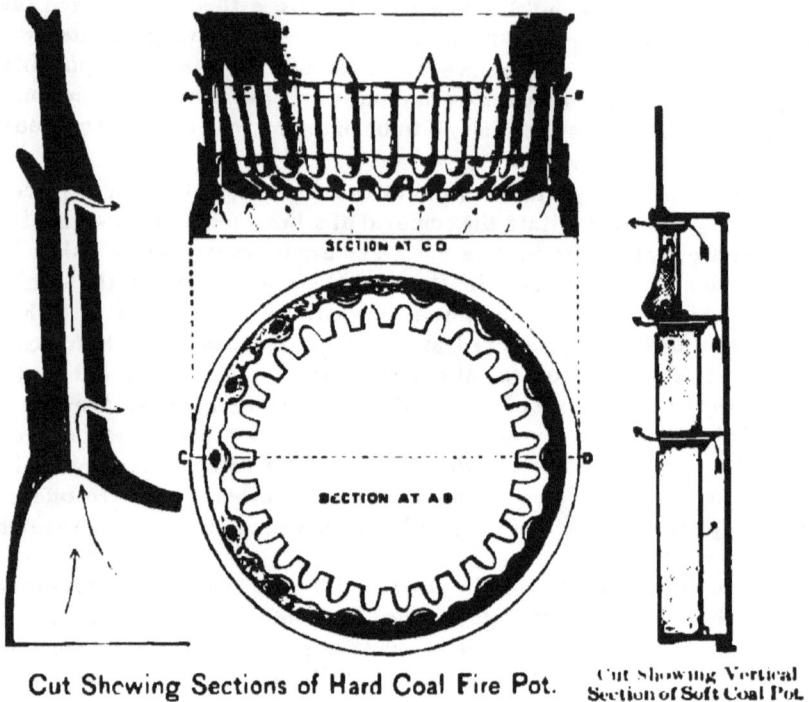

Cut Showing Sections of Hard Coal Fire Pot.

Cut Showing Vertical
Section of Soft Coal Pot.

Cut Showing Horizontal
Section of Soft Coal Pot.

In September, 1886, we introduced a fire pot that combined all the advantages of both fire-pots before described: having found that we can obtain as perfect combustion of the gases, and can use either hard or soft coal in the same stove or furnace, by the simple regulation of the supply of oxygen, at the proper place. This is attained by an adjustable slide. This fire-pot is now used in *all sizes and styles.* When *hard coal only* is to be used, we leave out the division plate and adjustable slide, and this renders the hard coal stove easier to clear grate of ashes.

THE HESS "PURE AIR" FURNACES.

FOR use in schools and other large buildings we make the HESS "PURE AIR" FURNACES IN VERY LARGE SIZES, to burn SOFT COAL as well as *hard coal and wood*, and which have all the principles so successfully used by us in our Portable Furnaces and Heaters, together with such new improvements as seem desirable.

They are made entirely of CAST IRON and of WROUGHT IRON and cast iron combined, or when preferred of CAST IRON and WROUGHT STEEL.

They contain from 24 to 84 air tubes, placed DIAGONALLY ACROSS the furnace *above the fire*, thus presenting an *unusually large heating surface* where the hot products rise, but far enough above the coals to avoid injury to the tubes or to the fresh air passing through them. These air tubes are so large and so admirably placed that an immense quantity of air passes through them from both sides of the furnace. We find that this method of placing pipes gives much quicker and better results than any mode in use.

It must be readily seen that these furnaces are able to deliver a much greater amount of warm air into a room than can be done by any other kind of a furnace or system of heating.

The oxygen to burn the smoke is supplied by an opening above the grate leading to a space behind the iron lining, where it becomes *superheated*, and is thence fed to the smoke through perforations in the linings, spreading over the coals in a spray, making a PERFECT GAS and SMOKE BURNER, filling the furnace with CLEAR HOT SMOKE AND COKE. The smoke is taken from an outlet at the *base* of the combustion chamber, where it is coolest. The result is a *great saving of heat* which would be lost up the chimney from furnaces of other makes having diving flues or direct outlets, which make the smoke pipes and chimney *so hot* as to set the building on fire. Such an occurrence is *absolutely impossible* with the Hess Furnace.

These furnaces are made in *five* sizes, from six to 14 feet long, and may be had either *portable* or *brick set*. The shape of the roof or cap is such that the heated air passes on into the hot air pipes *direct to the registers without an elbow or turn*, which is a great gain. They are simple, easily managed, HAVE NO FLUES THAT REQUIRE CLEANING OR SWABBING OUT. Should a brick, grate bar or air tube become injured it can be replaced by any handy man and WITHOUT TAKING THE FURNACE APART OR DISTURBING THE WALL OR TOP. All joints are made double and cemented, warranted gas proof. SOFT COAL SCREENINGS burn excellently well, the smaller size requiring two bushels to fill to run half day, and but one large shovelful per hour for the other half day.

The arrangements for hard coal is somewhat modified in the grate bars and brick, and the blue flame from the burning gas and smoke rises from one to two feet above the coals. For wood, the pot of No. 80 is made for 30-inch wood, and all others for four-foot lengths, and in that pot we save the heat from the gases and smoke also.

We use "Rocking Grate Bars" as the best we know of for large steam boilers or large furnaces. They break up the coke and clear out the ashes from entire fire surface. The firing becomes easy—the fuel gives off its heat to good advantage, and enables us to get more heat out of soft coal screenings and mine wastes. A door is placed at the end of the ash-pit for *clearing out the furnace into the ash-pit* by means of a long scraper.

BRICK SET AND PORTABLE.

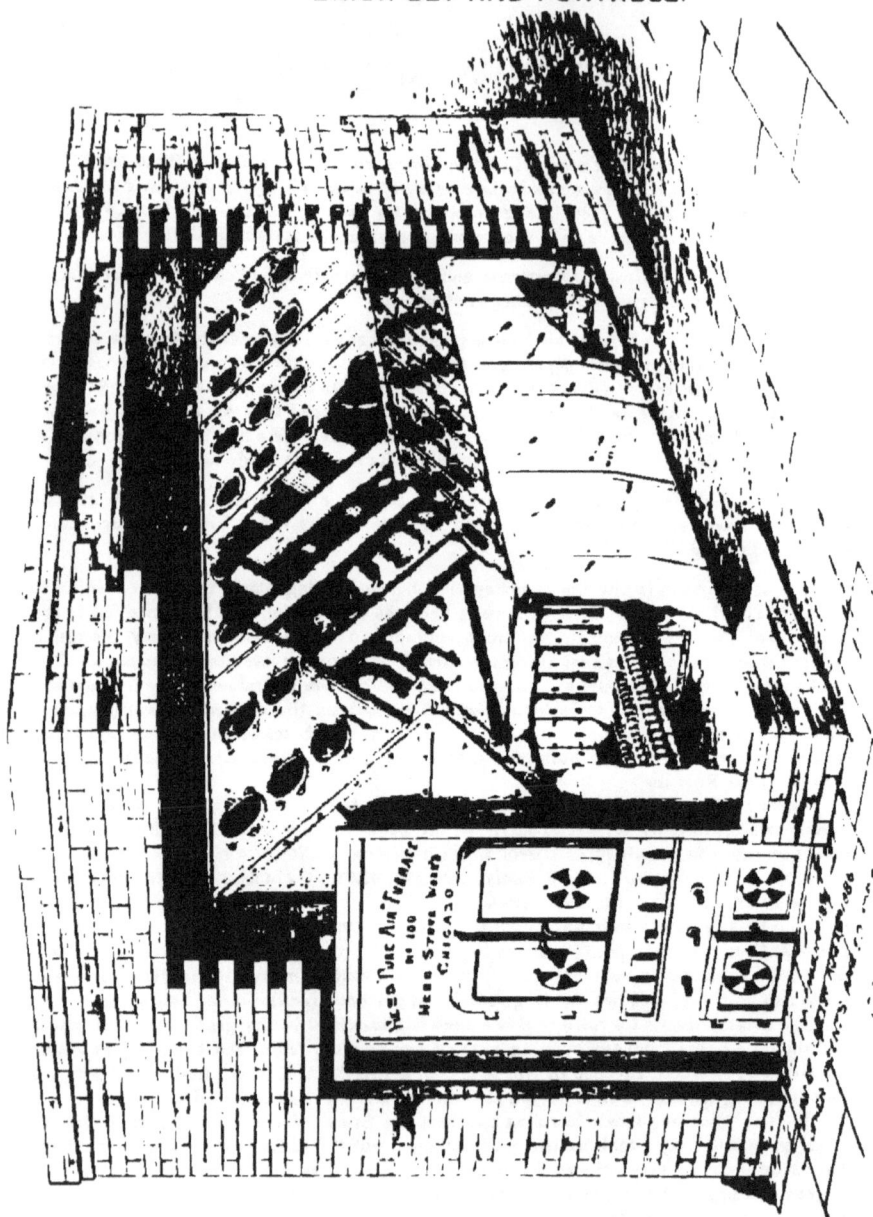

16

VENTILATION.

VENTILATION consists not alone in admitting pure air, but also in disposing of foul air, one act being as necessary as the other, and one absolutely depends on the other. It is one of the best aids in warming a house, and few places have any provision for it. "A house can be made to "breathe, to free itself of its spent and foul air and inhale fresh, as continuously "and almost as perfectly as do the human lungs." If a room be full of air it is impossible for more air to enter, unless there be an outlet for that already occupying the room. Provide a proper inlet and vent, and a change of air immediately takes place, and continues till the supply of air is exhausted or cut off.

In winter, when rooms are closed for warmth, ventilation is sadly neglected and the air becomes vitiated and often offensive. Cold air, being more dense than warm air, will settle to the floor of the room. This natural process is continuous, leaving the pure and warmer air in the upper part of the room. By placing an outlet near the floor we exhaust the cold and impure air, allowing the fresh warm air to enter, which rises, diffuses and settles to the floor and in its turn is removed. The circulation is kept up, and the supply of fresh air, warmed before entering, is continuous, affording a healthful, pleasant atmosphere. To remove the air from the upper part of the room is a mistake; it exhausts the heat without disturbing the foulness near the floor. The *outlet* for bad air should be *equal* in size to the *inlet* for the pure air.

But, to cause one body of air to flow in and to displace another body requires *force*. *Heat is force.* Heating an upright tube or flue causes the air within it to rise. The Hess heaters and furnaces have from 6 to 20 upright tubes in each. We take cold air from out of doors, warm it, and send it to the rooms in great volumes. The result is that it *fills* the house with warm air and exert such *force* that the pressure in the rooms will be outwards, causing the warm air to rush outwards through every opening or crevice, instead of allowing the cold outside to enter. Open a window on the leeward side, and instead of cold air entering the room, the air will rush out.

The amount of pure air needed for an ordinary ten room house requires an inlet not less than twenty inches square, which should open on the side of the house that gets the prevailing winds, usually the *west*. If properly constructed it need never be closed. It must take a furnace or heater having extraordinarily large radiating surface to heat such a volume oi air when the weather is 20° below zero, but if the house is properly built, and furnace, pipes and registers of the right size, correctly located, with suitable ventilation, the work is easily done and at less cost of fuel than by any other method. It will not do to try this method with ordinary make of furnaces, for they would not heat the air fast enough and you would freeze. We apply this system with a furnace placed in the basement, or by stoves in the rooms. In either case we obtain absolute equality of heat in all parts of the room. The floors will also be warm unless unprotected beneath.

To facilitate the escape of bad air the outlets should be connected with a chimney flue when possible, especially if the flue be warm. When this cannot be done, a pipe of wood or metal running from the floor through the roof will operate; or if a large audience room is to be ventilated, carry the smoke in a pipe of iron or fire-clay through the center of a large ventilating shaft. This will increase the upward flow in the shaft. This method has been in use many years, and is *not patented*. It is easily understood, and is reliable, if properly done—though it often fails through ignorance or carelessness in construction. Location, dimensions, connection with minor details are important. Letting the the air loose under floors is *seldom reliable*, as we have frequently found in School Buildings using this system. *Ducts should always be provided, and as short and direct as possible* to reach the flue, and no attempt should be made to carry the air downward below the floor joist.

Nor is the heat from a smoke flue a necessity to make a foul air shaft *draw*, but if the foul air duct is made of metal or smooth wood, placed in a partition that cannot become cold, and the duct continued out through the highest part of the roof, it will operate satisfactorily. A plan of both methods is shown in the illustration on page 15. When no shaft can be had, a simple and very effectual escape of cold air at the floor may be made by carrying escape ducts below the floors to the basement, and thence out through each wall, with automatic valves that will close on windward side and open on leeward side. The simplest and most perfect ventilator for the removal of bad air is an open grate. Ordinarily this is a grand contrivance for disposing of fuel. For an open fireplace, capable of heating as well as ventilating. See pages 28 to 33.

The Hess|"Pure Air" Furnaces and Heaters are so constructed that heat and ventilation are secured at the same time. They have such immense heating surfaces that they are always able to properly warm and deliver large volumes of air. The result is a most delightful, refreshing and invigorating summer atmosphere in your homes or in your halls and schools in the coldest days of winter. The perfection of artificial heat is attained.

Our "Dry Closet" System.

CORRECTS the objections found in other methods of ventilating Closets, Privies, etc., which require a constant fire—summer as well as winter—at the base of the ventilating shaft, for when the fire ceases to burn, the stench and bad odors are invariably carried to the rooms above. With our system this escape of odors into the rooms is *absolutely impossible*. We dispense with a stove or any artificial heat at the vent shaft, and consequently save all this great cost and care. It is automatic; perfectly reliable at all times and does *not* require the services of a janitor to operate. It is fully guaranteed to be efficient, and where our system of heating is used, no charge is made for the use of our "Dry Closet" system. The cost of construction is very light. When artificial aid is desired, we will furnish calorimotors for gas, coal, etc., at small cost.

Descriptions, diagrams and details will be given on application. Its use is strongly advised in schools and all buildings that have either water or Dry Closets under the same roof.

Hot Air Equalizing Register.

C. H. HESS, PATENT.

IT is well-known that the warmest air of a room remains at the ceiling and the coldest air at the floor, unless some artificial means are used to make a change.

It can be done, in a great measure, by proper methods of ventilation. It is also done by the tubes in the Hess Heaters, as shown on another page. It can also be accomplished by stirring it or "mixing it up."

We now propose to stir it up, circulate and equalize it by this Hot-Air Equalizing Register, so that the colder air of the floor may be warmed and lifted, and sent up to the ceiling along with the hotter air from the furnace, and thence distributed to the farther sides of the room, thereby creating a constant circulation of the air. This accomplished, no one will suffer from cold feet, and all parts of the room be warmed alike and upon the same principle as is so successfully used in the Hess Heaters.

In construction, the hot-air pipe from the furnace is carried up a short distance through and above the floor, into the body of this Register, which, being larger, allows an open air-space between it and the hot-air pipe. The heat of the pipe, and the expulsive force of the heated air causes the air at the floor to flow in this open air space, and to mingle with the air from the furnace, and to discharge together through the top of the Register. As this action is continuous it follows that *all the air of the room must become nearly uniform in temperature, whether the ventilation is perfect or not.* In fact, its operation is entirely independent of ventilation. It will be readily seen what an admirable invention this Register is for schools and large audience rooms.

RULES FOR PLACING A FURNACE.

1. Select a size of *greater* capacity than is actually required, that it may be run light, save fuel, and have *reserve power* for extreme weather.

2. Locate it as nearly as possible to the *center of the rooms to be heated*, that the heat may be distributed equally.

3. When possible, place the registers on the side of the room nearest to the furnace, that the *pipes may be short and straight*. The air moves slowly in *long* pipes and in elbows, on account of the *friction ;* therefore :

4. Use round elbows and large pipes. You can deliver more air or water through a large hole than a small one. For a bath room use eight-inch; small bed room, nine; ordinary hall and parlor, ten-inch; sitting or dining room, twelve; larger rooms in proportion. The registers should be in proportion to the pipes.

5. To reach the upper stories, the pipes or " stacks," as they are termed, are usually placed in the partitions, where they may be concealed. To be safe against fire, they should be *double*, with three-eighths of an inch *air-space between*, and *thoroughly braced to keep them apart ;* the joints double-seamed and soldered. This stack work and its branches cannot be too carefully done. The sizes for small bed rooms should be not less than 4x12, and large rooms 6x14. Round and oval stacks deliver better than flat or thin stacks.

6. Register boxes should be *double ;* or, if single, the wood work *should be lined with tin.*

7. The cold-air supply should come through a duct on or below the cellar floor from a *cold-air room* on the *windward side* of the cellar, with an open window to fill it. If this window is closed, the air should then be taken from the house into this room or duct. An ordinary ten-room house should have a room for cold air 4 to 6 feet square and an inlet 2 feet square. The duct also 2 feet square or its equivalent. While a pit under the furnace to admit air is desirable, it is not a necessity, as the air can be taken in at the side.

8. In each room where there is a register, there should also be an equal exit at the floor for cold air, to facilitate the inflow of warm air, especially when the doors are closed. These exits may be placed in partitions. Chimney flues may be used, if not otherwise fully occupied. An open fire-place will take care of two or three rooms if flue is large.

9. When the air is taken from the house these ventilators or exits are not needed, nor will they operate as such, but are liable to "draw down." It is always better to take the entire supply of air from outside, and if the furnace is of the proper size and properly put up, the window in the cold air room *can remain wide open in any weather.*

10. In heating a church or store, it is *better* to place directly over the furnace *one large register face* and border rather than two or more. Another face of equal size may be put in the floor, with a *return air duct* to the furnace, so that the air of the room may be heated over again. In a church this may be used while the room is unoccupied. In a store, with doors constantly opening the cold air room and duct is usually dispensed with.

11. The cold air openings and ducts should equal in area two-thirds of the combined area of the hot air pipes. The proper sizes for the cold air ducts of the Hess Furnace are as follows:

No.	5—5½-50, should be	. . . . . .	12 x 18 inches.
"	6—6½-60,	" " .	. 12 x 28 "
"	7—7½-70,	" " .	. 14 x 30 "
"	80—	" " .	. 20 x 30 "
"	90—	" " .	30 x 36 "
"	100—	" " .	. 30 x 50 "
"	110—	" " .	. 36 x 60 "
"	120—	" " .	. 40 x 80 "

or their equivalent.

12. When the outside air is supplied to the base of the Hess Heaters, as in schools, etc., the air inlet and the outlet should be as follows:

No. 1,	. . . .	4 x 4 inches.
" 2,	. . . . .	. 4 x 8 "
" 3,	. . . . .	6 x 8 "
" 4,	. . . . .	. 8 x 8 "
" 5,	. . . .	12 x 12 "
" 6,	. . . . .	. 12 x 18 "
" 7,	. . . .	14 x 20 "

13. As the success of heating by a furnace depends so much upon the proper arrangement, location and size of the pipes and registers, it is important that this work be done by those who fully understand it. We employ a corps of skilled workmen constantly on this kind of work. And as the piping will last a great many years, it should be of good material and the work be done in a thorough manner. We shall be pleased to offer suggestions if asked for, and to give estimates of cost on first-class work.

Cut showing mode of heating by a Furnace and Ventilating by Shaft containing Smoke Flue and also by Shaft without Smoke Flue

HEATING STOVES.

THE heating stoves are substantially like the furnaces, without the galvanized steel cases. They have the middle clinker-door for clearing the grate. Also a shaking and dumping grate. The vertical air tubes which perforate the combustion chamber *draw the cold air from the floor* and from adjoining rooms, warm it and send it back in great volumes, creating a rapid circulation of warm air, *equalizing the heat throughout.* The variation of temperature between the feet and the head is *rarely more than one or two degrees, and at the level there is none. This feature alone is worth the price of the stove*, and no one can appreciate the enjoyment of it until he has tried it. There can be nothing so good for use in schools, churches or audience rooms. As *every seat would be comfortable*, and because the cold air on the floor is *drawn away to the stove, no one suffers from cold feet.* In the home the children can play on the floor without taking colds. Plants can be raised and will flourish in any part of the house without danger of freezing. The ordinary stove makes those near it *too* warm, while those away from it are too cold. They are mounted in "Russia" iron and are made for all fuels.

Nos. 1, 2, 3 and 4 are made with oval cases, nickel-plated skirt, foot and top rails, handles and hinge pins.

No. 1 weighs 180 pounds; is 12x20x40 inches high. It has two tubes, will run all winter on *one ton of coal; eight quarts* will run it 24 hours. It will heat a room in 15 minutes; *will carry fire ten to twenty hours without attention.* Its simplicity, its beauty and its ready use commend it as a bed room stove for hotels and private dwellings. It will heat properly 1,500 cubic feet of space. *It will save its cost in one winter.*

No. 2 weighs 240 pounds; is 14x22x44 inches high. It has four tubes; it has double the capacity of No. 1; will use from one to one and a half tons hard coal per winter, or two tons soft coal. It makes a splendid dining or sitting room stove; will heat properly 2,500 cubic feet of space in any weather.

No. 3. weighs 350 pounds; is 16x26x56 inches high. Has six vertical tubes; fire-pot holds one peck of coal. This is the best size for "a family stove." Place it in the sitting room and it will warm two other adjoining rooms, equal in all to 5,000 or 6,000 cubic feet, to an even heat, and will use from one and a half to two and a half tons hard coal, or its equivalent in other fuel. It is also an excellent office stove.

No. 4 weighs 450 pounds, is 19x30x68 inches high; has eight tubes; will take care of 9,000 to 12,000 cubic feet. Has proved a satisfactory heater for schools and for large offices. It is a good size for a *hall* in *private houses,* as its influence will be felt through the whole building.

N. B.—Outdoor air can be brought directly into any Hess Stove or Heater. Ventilation attachment to smoke pipes furnished when desired

23

Nos. 1 and 2, 1887,
For Hard and Soft Coal.

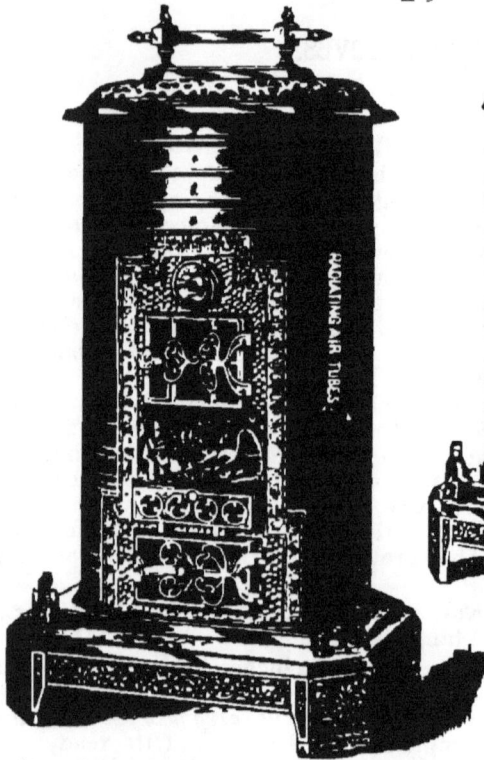

Nos. 3 and 4, 1887, for Hard and Soft Coal.

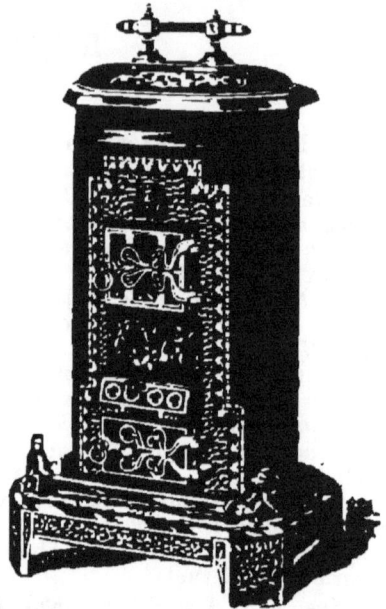

HESS
Pure Air
Ventilating
Stoves.
—
PURE AIR
Equalizers.

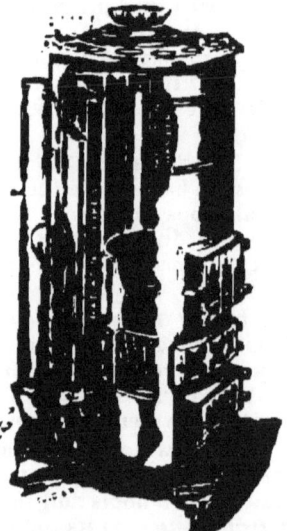

No. 1, 1884,   Price,
For Hard Coal Only. $17.00

No. 3, 1883,
For Hard Coal Only.

Hess Pure Air Ventilating Heaters.

Nos. 4A, 5-6-7.

For Hard and Soft Coal.

Pure Air Circulators.

The larger sizes, Nos. 4 A, 5, 6 and 7, have round cases and are quite plain, being the interior of the Nos. 4 A, 5, 6 and 7 Furnaces. They have great capacity, and are very serviceable for large rooms, schools, churches, stores, halls and factories. When placed near the main entrance, to catch the cold air as it comes in, they will make any portion of a large room very comfortable. While other stove makers have attempted to do the same, none have been able to get such satisfactory results.

All sizes of our ventilating Stoves and Heaters can be connected with out-of door-air.

THE FURNACE HEATERS

ARE constructed the same and of the same size as the furnaces of corresponding number, but with black cases in place of galvanized, and without a cap. Their advantage over the regular heaters consists in the entire absence of direct radiation, owing to the *double cases*, which allows seats or goods to be placed almost in contact—the radiant heat passing off in the circulation, and thereby increasing their capacity

N. B.—We guarantee, with any of our heaters of proper capacity, *to remove all frost from windows.* The sale of these larger sizes increases yearly for use in stores where a display of goods in windows has become a necessity in business competition, and no merchant who has experienced the benefits of them would think of using anything else.

The "Monarch" Tubular Steel Furnace.

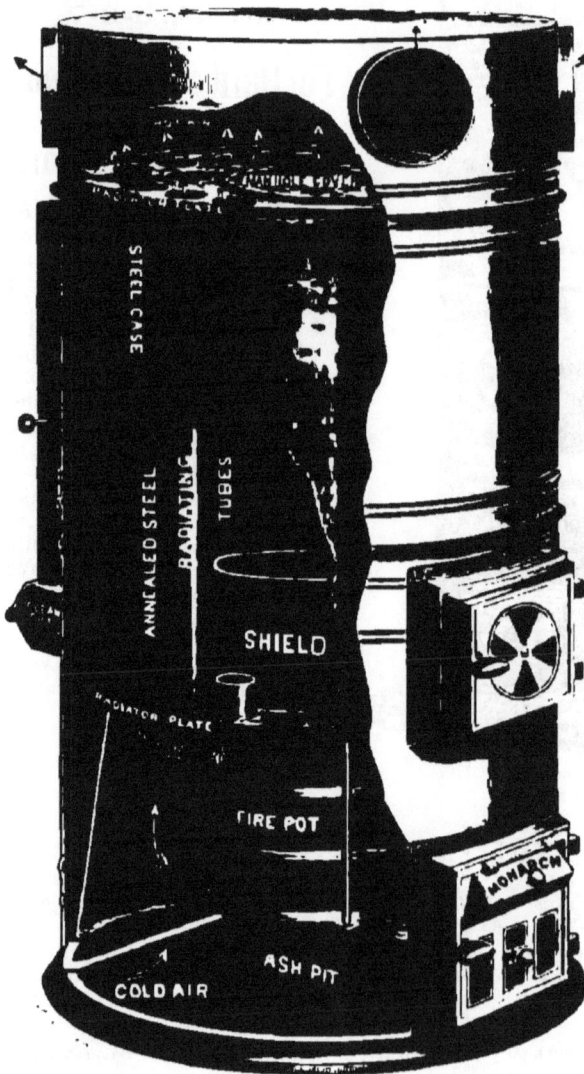

FOR HARD AND SOFT COAL

Powerful,
Economical,
Durable,
Low in Price.

Especially adapted to this severe Western climate, which is subject to sudden and extreme changes to cold with high winds, when a furnace is called upon to do its utmost in an emergency, and without consuming a coal mine in the doing of it.

IT HAS IMMENSE RADIATING SUR. FACE.

STEEL CASE

ANNEALED STEEL

RADIATING TUBES

SHIELD

RADIATOR PLATE

FIRE POT

MONARCH

ASH PIT

COLD AIR

Above the fire-pot, and in addition to it, is a large steel combustion chamber or drum, 28 to 40 inches in height, which is filled with 12 and 13 large vertical steel air tubes, surrounding the fire, in the same manner as in the Hess Pure Air Furnaces — which gives them their great power. Being made of wrought steel it radiates the heat rapidly. The steel is of fine quality, made expressly for our use.

All joints are made with double flanges filled with cement, to prevent leakage.
The fire-pot is large and heavy, in sectional rings, with straight sides, thereby preventing the accumulation and clogging of ashes; insuring equal combustion and good radiation from that portion of the furnace. The sectional construction of the fire-pot prevents cracking and consequent leakage. It also makes it more durable, as unequal expansion of the parts is not likely to occur.

Particular care has been taken to make these furnaces and heaters easy to manage. The fire-pot, grate and ash-pit are brought close to the front, so they are as accessible as the simplest stove. This feature is very seldom seen in furnaces. The grate is anti-clinker, shaking and dumping, simple in construction, and perfect in its operation. No machinery to it, and cannot get out of order. The ash pit is large. The furnace is cleanly, entirely free from dust or gas, easily controlled, and regulated to a nicety.

They can be relied on to do just what we claim for them. The prices are brought down as low as a good article can be furnished by any responsible manufacturer.

The Monarch Ventilating Heaters

Are made only in large sizes for use in Schools, Stores, Churches, Offices, Factories, etc. Their interior construction is like the furnaces; their exterior being a single case of American Russia Iron. In common with the Hess Pure Air Heaters, they possess this remarkable advantage over ordinary stoves and heaters, namely: They radiate but little near by, but send most of the heat upward through the steel air tubes and to the farthest sides of the room, drawing the cold air from the floor and supplying heated air in its place, making the floor warm, and all parts of the room of an even temperature. Thus they heat by circulation, all of the air of the room constantly passing through the heater. This feature alone is worth the price of the stove.

The outside air may be brought below the base of this heater, and by the proper arrangement for the removal of foul air, all portions of the room will become perfectly ventilated. Or a portion of the steel air tubes may take outside air while the rest are heating by circulation.

The Monarch Furnace Heaters

Are similar in construction to the Ventilating Heaters. They differ in having a double case, the inner one of steel, the outer one of American Russia Iron. There is less direct radiant heat, which allows the use of space close up to the heater

N. B.—We desire that no one should confound the "Monarch" Furnaces and Heaters, with the "Hess Pure Air" Furnaces and Heaters. There is a demand in a cheaper form, for goods containing some of the features which have made the Hess System so famous and satisfactory. And while we cannot claim the same economy of fuel, nor purity of the heated air that is obtained with the "Hess Pure Air" Furnaces and Stoves, the "Monarch Tubular" will prove more powerful and economical than the great majority of its competitors, and will be found in every way satisfactory.

There have lately been placed on the market many stoves, for which the same claim is made. But while the superior advantages of our methods are thus admitted, none have attained the Power, Efficiency and Wonderful Economy of the HESS SYSTEM.

PRICE LIST, AUGUST, 1887.

Monarch Ventilating Heaters.

Number.	Width. Inches.	Height	No. Steel Tubes.	Size of Fire-Pot Inside.	Cubic In. Combustion Chamber.	Square In. Radiating Surface.	Approximate Heating Capacity in Cubic Ft.	Size of Air Supply. Inches.	Kind of Coal.	Prices.
30	30	76	12	17 x10½	23 630	10.634	15,000 to 22,000	10x30	Range........	5 70
36	36	78	13	20 x12½	33,071	13.955	22,000 to 30,000	12x34	Small Egg....	90
43	43	79	13	22½x13	45,235	15.820	30,000 to 40,000	14x37	Large Egg....	105

Monarch Furnace Heaters.

Number.	Width. Inches.	Height	No. Steel Tubes.	Size of Fire-Pot Inside.	Cubic In. Combustion Chamber.	Square In. Radiating Surface.	Approximate Heating Capacity in Cubic Ft.	Size of Air Supply. Inches.	Kind of Coal.	Prices.
34	32	76	12	17 x10½	23 630	11 573	15,000 to 25,000	12x30	Range........	85
40	40	78	13	20 x12½	33,071	14.473	25,000 to 35,000	14x34	Small Egg....	110
45	45	79	13	22½x13	46,235	16 480	35,000 to 45,000	14x30	Large Egg....	130

Monarch Tubular Steel Furnace.

Number.	Width. Inches.	Height	No. Steel Tubes.	Size of Fire-Pot Inside.	Cubic In. Combustion Chamber.	Square In. Radiating Surface.	Approximate Heating Capacity in Cubic Ft.	Size of Air Supply. Inches.	Kind of Coal.	Prices.
53	53	80	12	17 x10½	23 136	10.698	12,000 to 15,000 or 5 to 6 Rooms.	12x30	Range........	80
40	40	80	13	20 x12½	33,384	13.050	15 000 to 30,000 or 6 to 8 Rooms.	14x34	Small Egg....	105
45	45	80	13	22½x13	45 290	15 401	30,000 to 35 000 or 8 to 10 Rooms.	14x30	Large Egg....	125

The Height of Furnaces, etc., can be changed to suit.

These figures are conservative and not intended to be adhered to strictly, as location, arrangement, kind and sizes of buildings to be heated, must be taken into consideration, in all cases deferring to the best experience and judgment of parties doing the work. Our experience has shown us that parties buying a size larger than just enough, have had the most satisfaction and economy. This is true of all makes of Furnaces, Boilers, etc.

Special prices given on contracts. Discounts to the trade.

The Hess Ventilating Grate and Open Fire-Place
WITH FURNACE ATTACHMENT.
[PATENTED.]

For comfort, power, economy and elegance they have no equal. Lower in price than any competitor. Yield thrice as much heat. Consume but one-third the fuel, and hold fire all night. The only open fire-place heater that does not disturb the mantel, the wall or the floor, and is the only one with furnace attachment. It is the only one where the heat is not lost up the chimney.

CUT SHOWING STYLE NO. I AS IT APPEARS IN WOOD MANTEL.

Various styles of fenders can be used. No. 1 can be furnished with square corners also. Coal Basket, 19x10 inches. Frame, 30½ inches wide by 32 inches high. Opening required, 29 inches wide, 31 inches high, 17 inches deep.

THE warming of dwellings by *Open Grate Fires* has not been possible heretofor In cold climates. Always desirable, very delightful, an open fire has been too much t f a luxury for all to afford. Fuel enough to warm several rooms would be burned; but ninety per cent of the heat went up the chimney. Therefore, from necessity, stoves, furnaces and steam have become the main sources of heat, often leaving the rooms without ventilation, or with no escape for bad air or poisonous gases; as a result we find headache, nervousness, debility, weak lungs, consumption, etc.

It has been the object of the inventor to prevent this great loss of heat, to save and distribute it where wanted, and to put it within the means of every man to heat and ventilate his house, that he, his wife and children *might breathe pure, wholesome air* and enjoy the "laughing fire on the hearth."

The ordinary grate is a good ventilator, but gives *direct* radiation *only*, and if the chimney has a strong draft, it carries off not only most of the heat, but causes *a strong current of cold air to come in through every crack and crevice.* In the "Hess" this is *changed*, the *colder* and impure air at the *floor is drawn* off and its place filled *with fresh pure air warmed to an even summer temperature.* This especially commends its use to invalids and persons with delicate or sensitive lungs.

In chilly days of Spring, Summer and Autumn, when the heat of a furnace or steam would be too great, the *"Hess" Open Fireplace is always ready*, and will make its influence felt in *every part of the house*, on account of its circulating power and heating capacity. In extreme cold weather our experience has proven that with the furnace attachment, heating by it *costs less than by ordinary stoves and furnaces.*

STYLE No. 2.

Coal Basket, 19x10 inches
Frame, 30½ in. wide, 30½ in. high
Opening required, 29 in. wide, 30 in. high
Depth required for Grate, 12 in
" " Furnace Attachment, 17 in.

Every "Hess" Grate has a *Dust-Flue*, which makes it *cleaner* than other grates. An Ash-Dump may also be used to drop the ashes into a pit in the cellar. When desired to heat an upper room a hot-air pipe may be carried up inside the smoke-flue. (See Cut).

Out of door air may be brought in at "A" or "B," as shown.

New Styles.

THE 1886 styles,
Nos. 2 and 3, are
the handsomest and
most artistic fireplaces
in the market. Either
size may be used with
coal-baskets or and-
irons. All have orna-
mental cast-iron backs,
over which air is con-
stantly passing, thus
rendering them inde-
structible.

STYLE NO. 3.

Coal Basket, 24 x 11 inches.
Frame, 30½ inches wide, 30½ inches high.
Opening required, 29 inches wide, 30 inches high.
Depth required for Grate, 9 inches.
Depth required for Furnace Attachment, 18 inches.

Construction of Fire-Place with Furnace Combined.

Behind the Grate is placed a *Small Square Furnace*, into which the smoke discharges; the outlet for smoke being at the bottom of this furnace, to prevent the escape of the hotter portions of gas, smoke, etc., which being light are held in the upper part until they part with their heat, when they settle to the bottom and are drawn out by the draft of the chimney. This Furnace is made entirely of *Steel and Cast Iron*, and upon the same principle as our regular Heaters and House Furnaces, being filled with vertical air tubes which become hot by the smoke surrounding them, and thus draw the cold air from the floor or from out of doors (if connection is made), warm it and send it through the upper Register of the Fire Place into the room. This creates a *constant circulation or distribution of warm air to all parts of the rooms, of course equalizing the temperature.*

Between the fire back and the Furnace is a space of two inches through which a current of air is also constantly passing, thus absorbing in addition all the heat from *back of the fire.* Thus it must be seen, as *we get the heat of direct radiation in front of the fire, the heat back of the fire, also the heat that is in the smoke, we must furnish a much greater amount than if it was absorbed by brick or lost up the chimney.*

For Sitting and Reception Rooms, Halls, Dining Rooms, Parlors, Hotel Reading Rooms and for heating Apartment Houses, they are superior to any other kind of device, as they can be relied upon for heating in any weather and all emergencies, and will hold fire over night as well as a stove.

THE appearance, construction, and operation of the " HESS " VENTI-
LATING GRATE are *identical* with the ' HESS ' Open Fire Place,
except the former *has no furnace behind* it to receive the smoke before
it goes into the chimney. The air passes *behind the fire*, and the *heat at the
back is saved* also the direct radiant heat. It is excellent for Bed Rooms,
Sitting Rooms, Dining Rooms, etc. It will do double the work of an
ordinary grate fire on less fuel, and is fully equal to the best Fire Place
Heaters and Ventilating Grates in the market.

BACK VIEW OF "HESS" VENTILATING GRATE.   INSIDE VIEW OF GRATE WITH FURNACE ATTACHMENT.

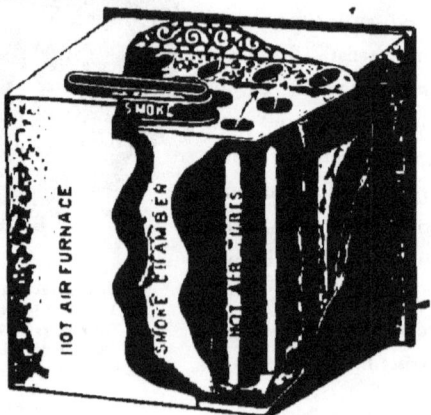

PRICES.

THE PIPE AND REGISTER FOR HEATING AN UPPER ROOM, $10.00.

Directions for Setting and Operating.

Ordinarily, the space between the face of a mantel and the back of the flue is from 18 to 24 inches and is filled up with brick and mortar to set the common grate. This is to be removed to a depth of 17 or 18 inches from the face of the mantel. The mantel usually projects 6 to 8 inches in front of the chimney breast, so there will always be found depth enough. The opening should be 29 inches wide, and the height for No. 1, 31 inches; for Nos. 2 and 3, 30 inches. The ventilating grates require the same opening though less depth.

The edges of the bottom, sides and top of the Galvanized Iron Case should be sealed with Plaster of Paris to insure against leakage of air, which would affect the chimney draft on the fire.

Any kind of fuel may be used. If hard coal, get range size. When the room is too hot, or when you desire to have a slow fire or hold fire over night, *pull out the ring handle* at the side. The under edge is notched and will stay at any point desired. This opens the door of the dust flue below the basket and *checks the draft.* In raking the fire or taking up ashes, if this door is opened, the dust will be carried up the chimney, thereby ..aking this grate as clean as a stove. Every year the dust flue should be cleaned out through the door with a small scraper.

Cut showing Cross Section of Grate with Furnace Attachment Hot Air Pipe to upper room, Cold Air Inlet and Ash Dump.

THESE BEAR WITNESS.

CHICAGO, MAY 10, 1880.

We like your Open Fire Place very much. For *health, comfort and cheerfulness* *it is grand.* My family have had almost perfect health since their introduction. by reason of the *pure air* and *even* temperature through the house. Invalids and those subject to headaches, from impure air, will find positive benefit in the use of your Open Fire Places. LEMUEL C. GROSVENOR, M. D., 185 Lincoln Avenue.

August, 1888.

Dr. Grosvenor tells us he has always heated nine rooms with three grates (with No. 3 Pure Air Heater in the hall to use only in extreme weather) at a cost of $45 per annum for fuel.

CHICAGO, July 10, 1881.

After five years constant use of your Open Fire Places, we unqualifiedly en-dorse all you have ever claimed for them. We believe they are the *best of the kind* in the market, and we shall take pleasure in telling every one so who may inquire of us. It uses a hod of coal per day. H. S. & F. S. OSBORNE, Attorneys. December, 1888—They continue to recommend the Fire Places.

Heman Baldwin. 3217 Groveland avenue, says: The longer I use your grates the more I enjoy them.

W. D. Gibson, 745 Washington Boulevard says: "It's a powerful heater."

That Fire place of yours is the finest thing of the kind I ever saw. J. F. WARD, with C. M. HENDERSON & CO.

I am much pleased with it. SAMUEL WEST, Hyde Park.

We are all delighted with the Fire place. It heats the two rooms delightfully. CHS. R. SHREVE, Supt. of Instruction, Martins Ferry, O.

Since the above was written, Mr. Shreve has had five more for self and son.

Dr. Stephen Breden, Franklin, Pa., says: "The grates are highly satisfactory. The addition of open air supply is of incalculable value, as it furnishes the lungs air, fresh and well ozonized."

T. T. Morford, agent of Union Steamboat Co., says: For years I have used your grate. It's a dandy.

C. W. Marsh, of Marsh Harvester Co., Sycamore, Ill., has used a Hess Open Fire place in his private "Den" for eight years.

The Verdict of all is: That the Ventilating Grate does twice the work of a Common Grate. The Furnace attachment does the work of a stove and on less fuel than ordinary stoves.

THE HESS COOKING RANGE "ECONOMY."

THE MOST COMPLETE SUMMER AND WINTER COOK STOVE IN THE WORLD.

IT burns wood, coal, coke and corn cobs—five cents worth for all day. In four months it saves enough to pay its cost. You may have your kitchen cool in summer and warm in winter.

The best cook stoves known consume more fuel and produce more heat than can be utilized, the greater part going up the smoke flue. They also make the kitchen and all the rooms above it too warm for comfort. Many a housewife becomes worn-out prematurely by working in a "red hot" kitchen.

By the systems in use in all the Hess Stoves, Heaters, etc., one has *absolute control* over the heat produced, as the engineer has over his engine; yet the stoves are so *very simple* and *easily managed* that any child or inexperienced person can run them.

We take the smoke out from the bottom of the stove, thus preventing the escape of the heat up the chimney; for heat, being the lighter, remains in the upper part of the stove, while the smoke, being the heavier portion, settles and passes off in the draught. We prevent the escape of heat through the sides of the stove by surrounding it with non-conducting walls—two inches thick—on the refrigerator plan. To this is added the burning of gases and carbon contained in the smoke by admitting oxygen to the fuel at the point of combustion; consequently the heat is *intensified*, the *fuel saved*, the *room kept cool*, and the fire held

G. H. HESS, Pat. Feb. 18, 1879. Oct. 4, 1881. March 4, 1883.

many hours without feeding, and every kind of cooking done more rapidly than by any other stove. The bake oven is portable and has non conducting walls enclosing it to retain the heat. *It is a splendid baker;* quick and ready for use in five minutes after starting a fire. Meat and poultry can be quickly browned on the outside so as to retain the juices and make it sweet and tender.

With this stove there is no need of another. It will do the work of *any four oil* or *gasoline stoves*, keep the *room as cool*, at less cost for fuel. It works *quicker* than they, and with wood or cobs, it is sooner out of the way.

By using flat-bottomed sauce pan upon the top of the stove lids, as shown in the cut, as much work can be done upon the No. 9 "Economy" as upon ordinary cook stoves with their heavy iron pots and kettles. Size of top is 17x28; total weight, 150 pounds, complete.

We connect *hot water attachments* for the bath and reservoirs for hot water. *By the aid of the bake oven the kitchen can be kept warm in the coldest weather.* Two and a half to three tons hard or soft coal, or one and a half to two cords hard wood, or cobs from three acres of corn, will run the No. 9 one year.

No. 9 is the best size for coal It will keep fire over night and will be in good condition for business for months together with very little care, which is of especial advantage in winter to keep the kitchen warm and *save* the *daily kindling of fires.*

We furnish reducing rings to No. 9 to fit eight-inch furniture without charge. The coal fire-pots are round; cast in one piece; made like a crucible; surrounded by air to help preserve it and to supply oxygen through the small holes near the top to the fuel, to burn gases and carbon contained in the smoke. The fire-pot for wood is oblong, though wood or cobs can be used in the coal fire-pot.

No. 8 is exactly like No. 9 except in size, being very little smaller, therefore little less capacity, but is an excellent stove, especially for wood and cobs.

These cuts represent the "Economy" and "Double Quick" with cooking utensils and oven removed. The oven to the "Double Quick" is to be lifted off or on. The oven to the "Economy" may be easily swung around on brackets, when not in use, and will be found convenient for setting things on top or inside.

THE SUMMER COOK STOVE. "Double Quick."

Burn, Wood, Coal, Coke or Cobs

FIVE CENTS WORTH RUNS IT ALL DAY TO DO THE COOKING, BAKING, WASHING AND IRONING FOR A FAMILY

It saves its cost in three months.

NO OIL! NO SMELL!

It is quicker and safer than oil or gasoline stoves, and has both come the business capacity.

It is made on the same principle as the "Hess Cook Stove, Economy," only smaller and cheaper. By its refrigerator case the kitchen is kept perfectly cool. Let it out and you can warm the room by it. It is a splendid baker. First rate for light housekeeping, and for quick meals. A capital laundry stove.

It is worth twice its cost for washing and ironing done, as it will boil four pails of water in 30 minutes and heat flat irons to keep two women busy. Good stove for camping out.

N. B. We also make light **Sheet Iron Stoves** for camping out, also **Campers' Cooking Outfits**. Send for circulars.

If Oil or Gas Stoves are wanted, send for circulars.

AUNT MARY'S BROILER.

This Double Wire Broiler and Cover is the best we know anything about, and is well adapted to our stoves. It is **light** and **very easy** to **keep clean**. It is **strong** and holds the meat firmly.

With a quick fire the meat is **seared**, and all the juices retained. When broiling use the cover of the broiler and keep ash door and slide closed, and there will be no smoke.

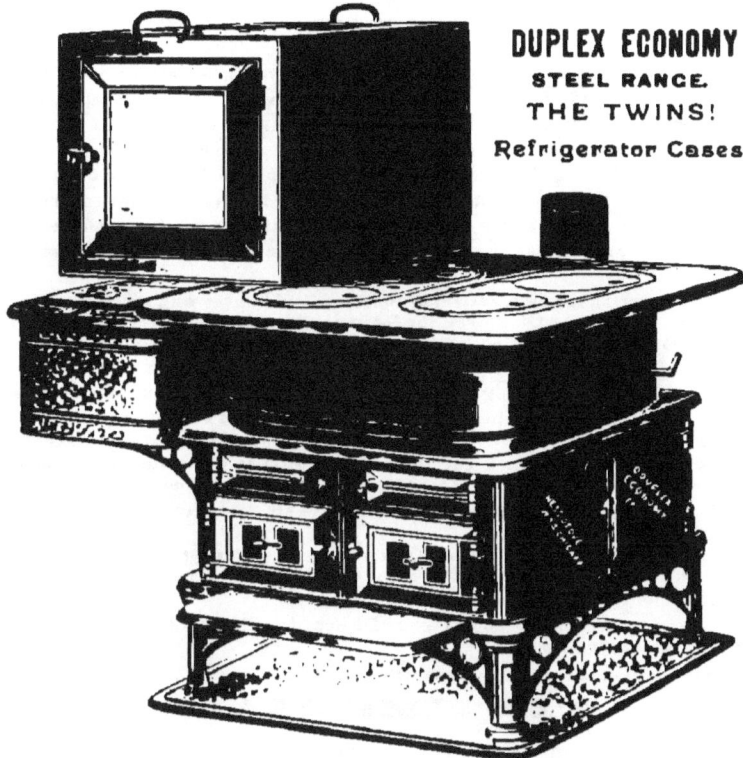

DUPLEX ECONOMY
STEEL RANGE.
THE TWINS!
Refrigerator Cases.

COMFORT.

SPEED.

While the No. 9 "Economy" and "Double Quick" were mainly intended for summer use, the majority of our customers have preferred to use the "Economy" as a winter stove also, on account of its good baking and quick cooking qualities, and its great economy of fuel; but there are occasions when extra work is required of a stove, and a greater variety of dishes to be cooked than can be done on a small surface. Hundreds of housekeepers have asked for a stove containing the advantages of the "Economy," but of larger size. The "Duplex Economy Steel Range" is made to supply that demand, being two No. 9s in one, making a Twin Stove. Each part in itself being complete and independent, having separate fire pots, baking arrangements and smoke outlets. Either half can be used separately or together, at will.

The Warming Closet and lower half of the "Duplex Range" is made of cast iron. The upper half has double steel cases. It contains the Hess patent gas burning fire pot, cast in two parts, and so arranged that new ones can be easily inserted. The oven is portable as in the single range. It has two cases of steel, asbestos lining and air space forming the best non conducting walls known to science. The water in the reservoir is heated by a wrought iron water back. The hot water back, for distribution, is a coil of wrought iron water pipe.

The Ash Pots are large. The arrangement for clearing the grate of ashes is good, very convenient and simple.

This Range possesses the following advantages over all other stoves, viz: a cool kitchen in summer, and a small fire easy to light and quick to work; it will do all the ordinary work of a family; runs at very small expense, and on account of the shape and construction of the fire pot is easy to run continuously for months together, and in winter will heat a kitchen as steadily as a heating stove. When extra work is required, the other stove is ready for use in a few minutes, thereby doubling the capacity. Thus you can have a slow moderate fire on one side, and a brisk hot fire on the other. Two persons can work without interfering with each other. Can cook on one side, and boil clothes on the other; can heat flat-irons on one side, and can fruit on the other; broil on one side, bake or roast on the other, without cooling the oven. In the common range or cook stove a large fire has to be built merely to boil a tea kettle, which makes unnecessary heat, and wastes the fuel, whereas, but one-fourth the heat and labor is required in this stove.

In comparing the Hess system of Summer Cook Stoves with other kinds, such as Vapor, Gas, Gasoline or Oil Stoves, the following advantages are readily seen: Where hot water is required for the bath, etc., or where there is heavy washing to be done, the Vapor, Gas or Oil Stoves cannot do it, or if attempted would take too long, or cost too much, and therefore the big range has to be started up, heating up the whole house. While Vapor stoves may do for light work, the Hess stoves are not only good for that, but they do the heavy work also, and as readily and as quickly as the regular coal stove. The smell of oil and gasoline is not the most agreeable in the world, and the house becomes tainted with it. With the best care in handling them, there is always a sense of danger, which no one is free from, and such stoves are used because the substitute has not been known.

The Hess Stove Works also make summer cook stoves for Oil, Gas, Etc., good of their kind, and have sold thousands, yet the fact is, that the persons connected with us, use, and prefer the "Economy" winter and summer.

We have used the "Economy" and "Duplex" for all sorts of work, and do not see how they can fail to please

TESTIMONIALS.

GEO. H. HESS CO.:   EAST SAGINAW, MICH., Aug. 4th, 1888.

Gentlemen—Every one who has seen your "Economy" Stove in operation is perfectly charmed with the way it works, and mother is so pleased with it that she says she don't see how she got along without one so long. She bakes home-made baking for a living, and it is such a splendid and rapid baker, it is just what she wants. I am certain I can make a good many sales for it.   GEO. A. SAVAGE.

GEO. H. HESS CO.:   October 2d, 1888.

Gentlemen—I purchased a No. 9 "Double Quick" Cook Stove some sixty days ago. It has been submitted to the severest tests by a number of parties. It does all your circular promises. It is the best Summer Cook Stove extant, and we propose to ignore a hundred dollar range we have, and use the little No. 9 "Double Quick" for winter, too, and have no doubt of its success.   REV, D. MILLS, Meade Centre, Kas.

December 6th, 1888.

We wish to give our unsolicited testimonial to the value of your No. 9 "Economy" Range. It is a splendid baker, and does all kind of work as well, and much quicker than any other stove we ever used. We have tested it thoroughly, and find it a success. We will use it both winter and summer.   TATUM & GORDON, Oakland, Miss.

May 20th, 1889, Mrs H. E. Starrett, of the "Weekly Magazine" says: "It does good work if it has half a chance."

February 18th, 1889.
I have been most anxious to communicate with you for over a year, but could not hear of you, although I wrote and asked others your address. I bought a stove of you in 1878, called the "Economy." I have found it a treasure, and through the kindness of a friend who gave me your address, I hasten to write to ask if I can get this stove repaired by you, and also to ask you to send me a circular of your new inventions and improvements. I should like especially to have a full and accurate account of the "Double Quick" stove advertised. Hoping you will give me a prompt response, I remain. Miss D. A. RICHARDSON, Fulton, S. C

March 16th, 1889.
I would like your price list of "Economy" Cook Stoves, as I think I can dispose of one or two more. My "Double Quick" stove works like a charm.
D. S. WOODWORTH, Portage, Wis.

A dealer writes us: "It takes well. One man has turned out his new $60.00 stove, and says it never will go back again."

"The best little stove I ever saw."
Mrs. R. M. AVERY, No. 39 Bryan Place, Chicago.

"The stove is a success. I feel as if I could not keep house without it. I am particularly pleased with the oven. Mrs. J. J. BROWN, Sheboygan, Wis.

Mrs. S. T. Wright used but one hod of coal in three days, doing all the work of her family. Nineteen loaves of bread were baked in three hours. Mail, Malta, Ill.

WILMETTE, ILL., Oct. 24th, 1882.
"I wish to add my unsolicited testimonal to the value of your No. 9 Cook Stove, out of my desire that every housewife should know, that simply as a matter of economy it is unsurpassed. On it I can do any kind of cooking, and as a baker, it leads any stove I ever saw. It is also a splendid heater, and will keep fire over night, and be ready for use the next morning. In short it did all the work I required of my range that I turned out, with much better satisfaction, and at less than half cost. My sister, Mrs. E. A. Slack, 1105 W. Jackson St., Chicago, says with me: "The longer we use your stove, the better we like it." Mrs. W. J. HOSMER.

"We think it excellent for light housekeeping. We have a nice range in same room, but seldom use it." FRANK C. POWER, of Woven Wire Mattress Co.

"My wife has had one of the Summer Cook Stoves for about a year, and it gives satisfaction." T. H. WHIPPLE, Detective Agency.

"My wife is enthusiastic in her praise of the Hess Cook Stove. I do not think I could improve it." M E. DAYTON, Patent Solicitor

"I am very much pleased with it." MRS. E F. MILLER, 33rd St.

"I found the little stove all you recommended and more. It is the best stove I ever used, and bakes lovely." Mrs. COMAS, La Grange.

DES MOINES, Iowa, Dec. 5th, 1887.
"I received the Cook Stove last Saturday, and am sorry to say that I am sadly disappointed and also deceived. It will not do anything you claimed. The fire-pot is entirely too small for anything. You claimed it would burn wood, coke or coal, and that is what I ordered, and it will do neither. In fact it is entirely useless to me." J. C. BURLACOTT

DES MOINES, Iowa, Mar. 1st, 1888.
"GEO. H. HESS & CO.,—Please pardon me for condemning your No. 9 Cook Stove as I did. The fact was, we did not know how to kindle it, until you sent instructions. We find it very easy to make a good fire. We have used it now about three months. Have used crushed coke all the time, and must say it gives good satisfaction. It beats everything I ever saw." Yours truly, J C BURLACOTT

READ THE TESTIMONY.

BURLINGTON, Ia., July 13, 1887.

I have been using your Nos. 3 and 7 heaters for two seasons. I consider them the *best in the world.* Mr. Hess has been the first to solve the problem of heating a house with pure air with the use of coal and iron. His ideas of heating and ventilation are far in advance of the age. JAS. A. GUEST, Pianos and Organs.

C. A. DUNHAM, Burlington, Iowa, one of the leading architects of this country says: From my long and unsatisfying experience with furnaces, steam and other systems of Heating and Ventilation I have quit recommending any but the "Hess", as I believe that to be the best extant and I fully endorse it. I have never heard a complaint—never knew it to fail, and don't see how it can fail. I have watched it for years.

S. S. BEMAN, Architect, Pullman Building, Chicago, June 22, 1887, says: The furnace furnished my house by your firm has given great satisfaction, and I take pleasure in testifying to its merits.
So say C. J. Warren and H. D. Deam Architects, Chicago.

University of Michigan, Ann Arbor, Mich., July 20, 1886.—The Hess Furnace has so many good practical points in its favor, and being constructed on scientific principles, it is really, in my opinion, the best Hot Air Furnace in the market to-day. PROF. M. E. COOLEY.

W. A. PENNELL says: I have had in my own residence in Normal, Ill., one of your Pure Air Furnaces, for two years, also one in my daughter's house in Chicago. Have also recommended them to several of my friends. From the experience we have had, I am free to say that your system of heating and ventilation gives us the most heat for the fuel used, and the best quality of heated air I ever experienced, and I do not hesitate to recommend it to all as far superior to anything of the kind in use at present day. For many years I was senior member of the firm of W. A. Pennell & Co., who were the first to introduce the Ruttan system in this country in 1867. Having had large experience in heating and ventilation, I think I know something of it.

In 1886, the Board of Education of Springfield, Ohio, desiring to get better methods of heating and ventilating—at the time using steam, stoves, various kinds of furnaces and "popular" systems of ventilation—adopted the "Hess" for the New High St. Building. Three large furnaces were placed in a battery, and the janitor, Frank Boyle, writes: "One furnace heats the whole house in moderate weather; when it comes colder, I run two of them, but last Monday was the coldest day we had, and I fired all three furnaces, and no trouble to have all my rooms to 70° and 80° by nine o'clock. Many rooms of several other schools in Springfield had to dismiss.

"I have been a janitor of public schools and public buildings for thirty years, and your system is the finest and most complete I ever handled, and I think I have fired all the best and most generally used."

In 1887, the Board of Education of Madison, Wis., erected a new High School and a Ward School. Not satisfied with any of the various systems they had in use, they adopted the "Hess" system, saving $1,500 in the cost of construction of the buildings. During the "blizzard" of January, 1888, the mercury dropped to 40° below zero, with high winds. All schools closed but those using the "Hess" System. Out-of-door air used. Ventilation perfect, and less coal used than any other system. Since then they have used it in another building, and nearly every member of the Board has adopted it for his private residence,—besides the Mayor and many citizens.

C. W. OSTRANDER, Janitor. Eureka, Ill., June 9, 1887. I have been using two Hess No. 80 and 90 in the Eureka High School building for two years, and can truly say they are, without exception, superior to any other furnace I ever saw. We have a large building, having six large rooms, a chapel room (as large as any other two rooms in house), two large halls, and six large cloak rooms, besides two large play rooms in basement, and the furnaces keep all the rooms at an even temperature of 70 degrees. I have tested them thoroughly, to see what they can be relied upon to do. When the thermometer indicated 25 degrees below zero, I have kept the rooms at 80 degrees all day. As for amount of fuel used, it takes from six to twelve bushels of soft coal for twenty-four hours. All the expenses for repairs we have been to in two years is $4, and that was for front lining.

CARROLLTON, Ohio, January, 1887. We, the undersigned, members of the Carrollton Board of Education, have had the "Hess Pure Air Furnace" placed in our Union School building; and do not hesitate to recommend it to all who are in need of a neat, healthy and comfortable heating appliance. GEO. J. BUTLER, JNO G. BYDER, J. V. LAWLER. D. O. RUTAN, Board of Education.
The undersigned, whose place is to be constantly about the school building, substantiate the above statement. A. W. FISHER, Principal, P. HAGERMAN, Janitor.
The School Board, of Hannibal, Mo., tried two No. 4 Hess Heaters in a building not satisfactorily heated by somebody's furnace. After one month's trial, bought six more. Since then they have adopted and put in Hess furnaces in their new buildings.

NEW BUFFALO, Mich., Oct. 4, 1887.
We have used three of your heaters in our Union School for two years, giving perfect satisfaction. For economy of fuel and uniformity of heat throughout the rooms, I have *never seen any other equal* to them. J. V. PHILLIPS, School Trustee.

Oct. 15, 1887.—A *fourth* heater has just been ordered by the same board. These heaters are also used by the Public Schools in many other towns.

Placing the Hess Heating and Ventilating system in the Chicago Public Library Reading room, 40 Dearborn St., in 1884, saved 18 tons of coal per winter and made and kept the air of the rooms pure and fresh.

SUTTON, Neb. Mollenaux is delighted with his Hess Furnace. It works to perfection. Says he has not burned more than 200 lbs. soft coal for 24 hours during the coldest weather and heats all the rooms in the hotel to 75 degrees, while at the school house with steam, they burn one ton of coal every 8 hours and could not raise the 2nd-story rooms above 45 degrees. J. F. SEARLES.

COURT HOUSE. METAMORA, Ill.

Date.	Temperature at 7 o'clock A. M.	Temperature of Rooms after one to two hours Firing.
February 2d, 1886.	14 deg. below zero.	Court Room, 95 deg. above.
February 3d, 1886.	21 deg. below zero.	Officers, 75 to 80 deg
February 4th, 1886.	20 deg. below zero.	Court Room, 80 to 90 deg.; Offices, 75.

Heated by two No. 50 Hess Pure Air Furnaces under vaults. I think the Furnaces a success, and I believe that they will do all that is required of them. I believe it will never fail to give entire satisfaction.
J. C. EWING,
Deputy Circuit Clerk,
Woodford Co. Ill.
R. HATCH, Oberlin, Ohio, Dec. 10, 1886.—We use a No. 6 Hess in the dining room (40 by 60 feet with 12 foot ceiling) at the Old Ladies' Hall; it is most admirable and satisfactory, especially in the astonishingly small amount of fuel needed, in always giving us fresh air, and never scorched or over-heated air, being entirely different from that of other furnaces, and in very satisfactorily equalizing the temperature of the room.

. Our system is used by the Washington Park Club, Rosalie Club, Kenwood Club.

GEO. M. KIMBALL ASS'T TREAS., Oberlin College, Oberlin, O., Dec. 10, 1886.—
I take pleasure in giving testimony to the superior merits of the Hess. 1st. It is
very simple in arrangement and adjustment, and therefore very easily operated.
2d. It is equally adapted to burning wood or hard coal. 3d. It is very prompt in
its action, so that on kindling a fire the heat is very quickly carried through the
house. 4th. It is constructed most fully in accordance with the laws of heat and
air, and therefore gives the largest amount of heat for the least amount of fuel.
5th. It is therefore very economical; last winter I heated my house of eight rooms
and halls thoroughly, day and night, with only eight tons of coal. 6th. A rare excellence is the quality of the air, which passes through the furnace so quickly that
it is not baked and burnt, as is the case with many furnaces. For these and other
reasons I can confidently recommend it to any wishing a furnace.

REV. M. J. WARD, RECTOR, St. Thomas' Church, Beloit, Wis., July 29, 1886.—
My church is 128x55, with 34 feet ceiling. Hess & Co. put in two No. 90 Furnaces.
They have given us the most perfect satisfaction. Unless the weather is 10 below
zero, we need to use but one furnace. I have had occasion to examine quite a number of different furnaces, and, so far as my judgment goes, I unhesitatingly pro-
nounce the Hess Furnace the best in the market. I have not met a more gentle-
manly or reliable firm to do business with. You can rely absolutely upon what
they say.

June 29, 1887: The furnaces continue to give us the most perfect satisfaction.
My people are delighted with the comfort they get from them. As for myself I do
not believe there is any better hot-air furnace made.

FATHER WM. MURPHY, Grafton, Neb., says: "I take a deep interest in the
Hess Heater. It is a beautiful application of natural science to the domestic hap-
piness of man. I have devoted years to the study of the subject. I feel proud of
your talent in this matter.

LA CLEDE Hotel, Grafton, Nebraska. July 30, 1887.—For two years I have
warmed the entire building with your furnace and the air both day and night
has been so pure and so different from other houses, that my guests have remarked
the fact. There has been such a decided saving of fuel, that I consider your furnace as one of my best investments, as it means comfort to my guests and economy to myself. B. T. LASUELL, Proprietor.

ARLINGTON HOUSE, Wausau, Wis., is heated by a No. 70 Wood Furnace. The
proprietor says: He has been in the hotel business 30 years and has tried steam and
all kinds of heating and the "Hess" is the best of them all.

REID, MURDOCK & FISCHER, Wholesale Grocers, Chicago, say, July 21, 1887:
We have used three of your Furnaces and Heaters, with your system of ventilation,
in our offices during the past four years. They have verified the prediction of your
Mr. Hess, by giving uniform satisfaction. We are pleased with the system and
your mode of doing business, and we believe that parties dealing with your firm
will never have cause to repent it.

C. W. AUSTIN, Manager for Adams & Westlake Mf'g. Co., 94 State St., Chicago,
says June 25, 1887: The No. 6 Furnace has proved satisfactory in every respect. It is
quick, effective, and economical, easy to regulate and hold fire all night. I put on
coal in the morning and regulate the dampers, and it needs no further attention till
night. I keep the temperature of my rooms at 74° to 76°, but, if necessary, inside
of ten minutes I can send the mercury to 85°. I am well pleased with it, and if I
was going to buy another one to-morrow it would be a Hess Pure Air Furnace.
The No. 7 in our store is equally satisfactory.

WM. L. POTTER, Superintendent North Chicago Rolling Mill Co., Chicago, says: I have been using your No. 80 Pure Air Furnace in my residence for nearly two years, and I find it to be perfectly satisfactory, it being a powerful heater and economical in fuel, free from gas, smoke and dust, and I can cheerfully recommend it to all who like a warm and confortable house in very cold weather.

[In April, 1887, Mr. Potter stated that his average coal consumption has been about ten tons of hard coal per winter. His residence is quite a large one.—G. H. H. & Co.]

CHANDLER & Co., Mortgage Bankers, also BARNARD & CALKINS, Real Estate, have used the Hess Furnaces for some years and continue to buy them in preference to all others. They say: "We can hold our tenants so much better than with any other heating we have tried, that it has proved to be the best investment for us. Tenants do not move when their homes are kept warm at small expense. Landlords make a great mistake in buying cheap furnaces."

The two furnaces I bought of you six and two years ago, I think are the best heaters and coal savers in the market. We have never used a furnace that required so little attention, and proved so durable. M. A. HAWKES, 108 Dearborn St., Chicago, 6 Aug. 1887.

We have used your Furnace for three years with perfect satisfaction. I do not think there is any better furnace made than yours. I can say the same of your Open Fire Place, which we have used for three years; we would not be without it for several times its cost. I recommend your Furnace and Open Fire Place as the best that has yet been made, in my opinion. HEMAN BALDWIN, 3217 Groveland Park Ave., Chicago.

LUTHER W. MCCONNELL, Credit Dept. MARSHALL FIELD & Co., Wholesale Dry Goods, has a No. 80 Hess Pure air Furnace and Mrs. McConnell says: "We keep our house so comfortably now in the coldest weather and through the warm days of spring can run a very small fire. It's a pleasure to say this after the bother we have heretofore had in attempts to heat our house."

I have used one in my house in Rogers Park for years, and it has never had to be repaired. I like it because it heats the house so quickly. F. C. MARKS, with Marshall, Field & Co.

W. K. SIDLEY, Buyer for Keith Bros. & Co., Hats, Caps, etc., Chicago, says, June 27, 1887: The furnace purchased from you two or three years since, and used in my home, No. 3823 Ellis Ave., has given entire and continuous satisfaction both in point of economy of fuel and heating capacity.

So says Thos. Caliger with same firm. Montgomery, Ward & Co. recommend it to all enquirers. Joseph J. Ward, with C. M. Henderson & Co., endorses the Hess Furnace.

ROBT. SCOTT (of Carson, Pirie, Scott & Co., Wholesale Dry Goods) uses the Hess Pure Air Furnace, and recommends it—so do their Cashier Henry Grassie and their Salesmen Wm. Grassie, John R. Towle, D. C. Dierdorf and others.

The furnace I put in my residence three or four years ago, I found to be very much superior to the one I threw out. It burned much less coal and I am very much pleased with it. JAS. H. SHIELDS, of Shields, Brown & Co., Chicago.

J. W. DRANT, of Drant & Hawtin, Wood Engraving, Chicago, says: I have had your Furnace in my house for three years, and it has given entire satisfaction. Quicker results can be got with a small amount of fire than with any of the old cast-iron Furnaces.

CHARLES E. BROWNE, Real Estate, Chicago, says, June 30, 1887: I find them all that they have been recommended to be. They give me perfect satisfaction, so much so, that if I wanted another Furnace I should unhesitatingly take one more of yours.

L. N. STRATTON, Prest., Wheaton Theological Seminary, Wheaton, Ill., says, April 25, 1885: The Furnace you sold me is capital. The smoke-pipe is barely warm. All the heat is saved. I have used the best of stoves, and had a pleasant experience with steam heat for years. This is better than either, for it brings in fresh air warmed, and forces the cold air down and out of the ventilators.

Both the quality of the heat and its comparative cheapness are to us entirely satisfactory, now, after more than three years' experience. O. F. LUMRY.
For thirty-one years Professor in Wheaton College, Ill.

L. C. COLLINS, Sn., Norwood Park, Ill., says, June 20, 1887: Having used one of your Furnaces in my own house two years, besides being familiar with two others in different dwellings, owned by members of my family, I take great pleasure in saying that they have given most unqualified satisfaction. I can recommend it to every one, both for heating and economy.

H. McALLASTER & Co., Advertising Cards, Etc., Winnetka, Ill., says, March 25, 1884: One of the redeeming features of the long, cold winter, has been our Hess Furnace, and it has become indispensable to our comfort. No difficulty in keeping perfectly warm when the mercury ranged from 20 to 30 degrees below zero; and in the early days of spring we maintain a delightful temperature. We have found the "Hess" reliable, accommodating itself to varying temperature, economical and easily managed.

J. O. Smith, C. F. Cook, Gen. M. D. L. Simpson, Mr. Jones, C. H. Winship and others in Winnetka say the same. At Highland Park are E. H. Denison, Schuyler M. Coe, Francis D. Everett, and, at all the Suburban Stations about Chicago, are men enthusiastic over the Hess Furnace.

JAS. B. GALLOWAY, Attorney, Chicago, says, June 25, 1887: I put one of your Furnaces into a cold frame house three years ago, and was told by my tenant that there was no day when the house was not from 75 to 80 degrees, and used less coal than where he had previously lived. I put a similar Furnace into another frame house two years ago, with similar satisfaction.

During 1888 Mr. Galloway has bought three more Hess Furnaces.

BENJ. F. NEWHALL, Glencoe, Ill., says: We heat nine rooms with your No.5½ Furnace. We burned fifteen tons of coal in the two seasons.

E. S. RICE, DuPont Gunpowder, Chicago, Ill., says, June 29, 1887: I take pleasure in acknowledging the intrinsic value to me of the Hess Pure Air Furnace.

CLEMENT, WILLIAMS & Co., Furniture, Milwaukee, Wis., says, June 30, 1887: We have used two of your Furnaces in our store for two years, and they continue to be perfectly satisfactory. With a very moderate amount of coal we heat our store in every part in the coldest weather. The building is 40x185 feet, four stories and basement (350,000 cubic feet). They are easily managed, have kept in good order, and we bear cheerful testimony to their merits.

We are very much pleased with the Furnace: it does the work splendidly, and while our neighbors are freezing we are very comfortable. All that have seen the Furnace are very much pleased, and we can cheerfully endorse it for you at any time. W. E. ELLIOTT, Chief Engineer, Goodrich Transportation Co., Milwaukee.

44

CHIEF ENGINEER's Office, C. & A. R. R., Chicago, July 10, 1887.—After three years' use, I think it cannot be beat. A perfect "Pure Air" Furnace. CYRUS J. CORSE, Norwood Park, Ill.

C. C. Warren, Hinsdale, Ill., says: The large portable Furnace I bought of you two or three years ago has given me satisfaction. I do not know of a better Furnace.

[N. B.—C. C. Warren was formerly of the firm of Cushing, Warren & Co., manufacturers of the "Cushing" Furnace.]

H. C. GOODRICH, Chicago, November 14, 1881 : Your furnace at my house gives better satisfaction than any of the three kinds before used the last twelve years, and I bought those which were considered the best. It consumes very much less coal, and I believe if the fire pot were broken to pieces, we could not possibly get any gas. The air is the pleasantest I ever knew to come from a furnace. Dec. 1888. Still in use and says it's the best.

CHAS. L. COREY, Engineer, Fire Department, City of Chicago, says: Having used your Pure Air Furnace for the last two winters with such satisfactory results, I feel impelled to congratulate you on your discovery of a perfect system of heating public buildings with pure air. Its principal good points being economy, comfort and neatness.

METROPOLITAN SAFETY FUND ACCIDENT ASSOCIATION. Chicago, June 28, 1887.—Last winter was the third year I have used your Pure Air Furnace. I have burnt one-third less coal than my next neighbor, who has a house a trifle smaller. A. B. SMITH, Adjuster.

I have used your Furnace four years. I think it the best and I have had a somewhat varied experience with Furnaces. My wife joins me in wishing you every success in selling people a Furnace that will "keep them warm" and still leave them a little money for something besides coal. J. C. WINSHIP, Printers, Chicago, June 25, 1887.

W. M. COULTER, Capitalist, says: In every respect it is a first-class furnace. It takes but 5 tons per winter and makes us much more comfortable than the one we took out which used 10 tons. Chicago, 21 June, 1887.

ED. R. SWETT, Atty., Chicago, Ill., June 25, 1887. Your furnace gives entire satisfaction. It does its work well, and is economical. I also found Mr. Hess very obliging in seeing that the furnace was properly set and in good working order. He seemed determined, at the cost of any amount of trouble, to give satisfaction and he succeeded completely.

The Hess Pure Air Furnace which we have had in use for two years, has done just what you claimed for it when putting it in, viz., heated our house from top to bottom, left us pure air to breathe, and was economical in the consumption of coal and easily managed. We selected your Furnace after careful study of, and comparison with the merits of others, and believed when we did so we were getting the best for our money. We have had no reason to change our opinion since. WM. D. Miller, 575½ Monroe Av., Hyde Park.

[Note.—July 17, 1887. Mr. Miller has ordered another Hess Furnace for his new house.]

I have used two other furnaces in my house, but have been unable to properly heat it until I purchased yours, which I am now able to do with less fuel than with the others. FRANK S. OSBORNE.

DARIUS FULLER, Real Estate says: The best heater of any Furnace I ever saw.

H. J. DAY, Grafton, Neb., says, July 12, 1887: I have one of your "Pure Air" Furnaces in my store and one in my house. They are all and more than you claim for them, and surpass my most sanguine expectations. I cheerfully recommend them for economy, cleanliness and pure air. You may say everything in praise of the Pure Air Heater.

BANK OF GRAFTON, Grafton, Neb., says, July 2, 1887: I have used it now for two years, and find it exactly as recommended by you. All over the house there is a uniform temperature, and is kept so with much less fuel than would be consumed in three base burners.   R. C. PRICE.

GEO. H. WARREN, Grafton, Neb., says, June 29, 1887: I have used one of your Furnaces in my house for the past two years, with the very best results. I have a large, cold house, and find no difficulty whatever in heating it during the coldest weather.

A. BURMESTER, Omaha, Neb., says, July 22, 1887: I have called on all persons where I have put in Hess Furnaces in Omaha, and found, in every case, they are well satisfied and highly recommend the furnaces. They do the required work with less fuel than any other furnace, and I feel proud in being able to say so.

The Furnaces in our church have proved very satisfactory. We are not only pleased with the Furnaces, but with the Company, for their fair and honorable dealing.   E. P. BARTLETT, Rector of First Baptist Church, La Moille, Ill.

ROBERT ELLIOTT, Trustee Public Library, Hannibal, Mo., says, July 25, 1887: The No. 80 Furnace in my residence has shown itself to be a powerful and economical Heater. My appreciation of it is hereby manifested by placing with you an order for a No. 90, to be set in our new building.

N. W. SHERMITT, Oberlin, O., says: The Hess Furnace warms our whole house of 28,000 cubic feet. We would not be induced to exchange it for the twelve stoves it would require to heat our house as well as the furnace does.

C. E. & C. M. ANTHONY, Bankers, Peoria, Ill., reported that the Hess Furnace which replaced eight or nine stoves in their house in Washington used very little more wood for the whole house than formerly their dining room stove required. They use the Hess in Peoria also.

A. C. TIEDE & Co., Millers, Elkport, Iowa, says: The heater is a success. The same amount of wood used in a stove which warms one room is sufficient to warm almost the entire house of eight good sized rooms. It exceeds our expectations.

H. M. BOWMAN, Cashier, Atlantic National Bank, Iowa, says: We are using the Hess Pure Air Furnace and with perfect satisfaction. Would not get along without it.

WM. H. COBB, Dry Goods, Tipton, Iowa, says: I have used the Hess Furnace two years and it is a perfect success. I heat a fifteen-room house with ease and comfort. It is very economical with coal.

JOHN A NASH, of Nash, Phelps & Green, Attorneys, Audubon, Iowa, says, June 30, 1887: Before I purchased I spent considerable time in the examination of the different Furnaces. I purchased the "Hess," and have congratulated myself almost daily during the past long and exceedingly cold winter on the wisdom of my choice. We have heated our entire house, consisting of eleven rooms and two large halls, every day during the past winter and never knew what cold weather was, with 9½ tons of hard coal. To my mind it has four incomparable points that should recommend it to everyone. First, it is simple so that any child can run it; second, the temperature of the entire space to be heated is even; third, economy of fuel, and last the atmosphere is always pure. I can and have unhesitatingly recommended the "Hess" as the best and cheapest.

N. T. BURROUGHS, First National Bank, Cherokee, Iowa, says, March 28 1887: Your Furnace has in every way filled the recommend. I like it very much.

JOHN M. WALLACE, Prest., First National Bank, Greeley, Col., says. July, 1887: We have in use four of your furnaces in our bank block, and they give entire satisfaction.

CLINTON HOWARD, Pana, Ill., says: I found it to possess all the merits that you claim for it.

EUNICE HOOPER, Pana, Ill., says: My Furnace works beautifully and is very economical.

NATHAN W. SMITH, Des Moines, says : The Furnaces I put in have given entire satisfaction.

FRED L. MURRAY, Agent C. & N. W. R. Co., Lake Geneva Station, says, June 24, 1887 : Your No. 6 Furnace has given the very best satisfaction, and to-day is as perfect as when first set. I heat my house from top to bottom on five and a half tons of coal, and run my fire six months.

CLARK & MARTIN, St. Paul, Minn., say, June 30, 1887 : We would not be without your Heater for double its cost. It saves fuel and the heat is so evenly distributed nothing can freeze. We kept lemons in our show window over night with mercury down to 30 degrees below.

I have used the Hess Stoves with Hard Coal, Soft Coal and Natural Gas. I have a Hess Heater No. 3 in my house. It is the *best heater* in *every way* that I ever saw or used. I have made, bought, sold and handled all kinds of stoves forty-three years. I ought to know something as to the quality of stoves in that time.
A. N. SMITH, Lima, Ohio.

"We have one in our office and two in our home and like them. The firm is reliable." FARM, FIELD & STOCKMAN.

"The Pure Air Heater is quite a luxury. It meets all the requirements." GUS. LATHAM, Heron Lake, Minn.

I consider them as near perfection as can be, and all you claim for them. E. C. LEWIS, Attorney, Juneau, Wis.

The No. 4 Hess Stove has heated seven rooms in my house all winter (coldest days, 49° below zero.) It's a dandy, and the best and most economical stove I ever used. E. L. POMEROY, Nashua, Iowa.

The perfection in heaters, the Hess Stove, stands ahead of all others. My No. 1 for which I paid $15 in December, heats two rooms and I save $20 in coal this winter. WM. B. BOWDISH, Morrison, Ill.

State University IOWA CITY, Ia., June 29, 1887. I most gladly bear testimony to the excellence of your stoves. They are about *the only thing I have ever found which realized the promise of the manifesto.* For two years I have heated three parlors and three sleeping rooms with the No. 4 stove, seldom using more than *two hods* of coal a day of twenty-four hours. I think it is doing more than you would claim for it. It is certainly the most wholesome, agreeable and economical stove that I know anything about.
E. M. BOOTH, Prof. Rhetoric and Oratory.

CHICAGO, March 18, 1887. Your Heaters have given us good service, and we consider them *first-class.*
DAVID BRADLEY MFG. CO.

Merchants Despatch Transportation Co. Chicago, March 17, 1887.

We are perfectly satisfied with the heater. The only heater we have had that has done the work wanted.

June 25, 1887.—We were never able to heat our office with two large stoves before your heater was put in, four years ago. *Yours has done it alone,* therefore I can say it is a perfect success. I am pleased to give you my opinion. We could not do without it. J. M. AUBERY, Agent.

Chicago, June 29, 1887.

We consider your heater one of the best investments we have ever made. We have used it three years and it has fulfilled *all the promises* you made for it. It has been a great fuel saver over all our former modes of heating.

Chicago Furniture Supply Co.

Chicago, Oct. 9, 1884.

We have used your No. 5 heater in this office, 35x40 feet, 12½ feet ceiling, for three years, using from four to four and a half tons coal per winter. In the coldest days the *heated air is the same all over the room.* It saves fuel enough to pay for itself every two years. Lumberman's Exchange. (By Secretary.)

The following lumber manufacturers use our heaters: Martin Ryerson & Co., N. Ludington Lumber Co., Kirby Carpenter Co., W. Ripley & Son, Soper Lumber Co., and others.

Lumber Trade Journal, July 1, 1887.

I have now had seven years' experience with your goods in my dwelling and office, and while I hear of other devices which claim to do as much work. I do not hear of any which will heat a *seven-room house from October to April with five tons of coal* as I have done for the past six years. George W. Hotchkiss.

Orr & Lockett, Hardware, Chicago, have used the heaters for seven years. They will have no other kind.

Kellogg, Johnson & Bliss, Hardware, Chicago, heat their large store, 48x190, with *one* No. 70 Furnace heater.

N. K. Fairbank & Co., Lard Manufacturers, Chicago, *took out steam* after using it for two years, and replaced it with *two* Hess Pure Air Heaters four years ago, and will use no other.

Kirby Carpenter Co., Lumber, Menominee, July 14, 1887.

I have used one of your No. 3 stoves for the past two winters. I would not exchange it for the best self-feeder ever made. • • • You may send me another one No. 2. Walter G. Buhlin.

There is nothing superior, if as good, for getting as large amount of heat out of coal and simplicity and ease of handling. C. C. Wallin & Sons, Tanners, Chicago.

Moll & Thomas, Leather, Chicago, give a similar report.

We have used one for two seasons in our store in Chicago, and can wish for nothing better. Hoffman Bros., Publishers and Booksellers.

The principle is right, the construction good, and its use very effective and economical. Eugene S. Pike, Chicago.

H. S. & F. S. Osborne say: "For several years we heated our three offices with a No. 3, and each room was kept at 70 deg., seldom more than two or three degrees variation."

W. A. Boatman, depot master, Union Depot, Chicago, says: "I seldom use my old furnace any more, except in very cold weather, as my Hess heater warms my whole house most of the time, and uses only one-third the coal, and I like the heat much better."

Father Tighe, of Catholic Church of Holy Angels, Chicago, had a furnace of the common cast-iron sort. Never comfortable. Put in a No. 70 Hess Furnace Heater in one corner of the church. That made every seat warm, those near were no warmer than those 100 feet distant. The same report comes in from all the churches where our heaters are used.

ADA, O., Feb. 24, 1865.

Your No. 3 heats twice the space on less fuel, with a pleasanter heat, than did our base burner—and we had a good one.
June 30, 1887.—We now use two of your stoves. They do all you claim for them. Will never use the old style stoves again. P. W. BEAM.

We use your No. 3. It is the "boss" stove. We would not take $50 for it.
MR. AND MRS. WM. CONNOR, Ada, O.

C. and N. W. R. R. Office, CHICAGO. Oct. 29. 1887.
I have used two of your stoves for several years. No. 3 heated my sitting room, one parlor and three bed rooms, using an average of two tons hard coal per winter, keeping all my rooms of an even temperature. In one alcove we had plants 15 feet from the stove and they bloomed nicely. The front parlor, 15 feet square, was heated by the No. 1 stove. It used an average of six quarts of coal for 24 hours; never exceeding 10 quarts. It holds fire nicely. Have kept it going 24 hours, without replenishing, in warm days. The fire in both stoves never went out from the first of November until the first of May. The temperature we kept all day and evening through the rooms to 70 degrees, and in the morning was never below 55 to 60. My house is frame, exposed on all sides. The stoves are in perfect order yet, and I cheerfully recommend them for giving the *best heat* and for warming all parts of the rooms evenly, and especially the floors. J. G. ELLITHORPE, Baggage Agent.

BEATRICE, Neb., Oct. 19, 1887.
The Hess Heating Stove is, in my judgment, the only perfect system of store heating. S. W. WADSWORTH, Jeweler.

E. Prouty, Guns, etc., 53 State Street, says: "For years I bragged on the Stewart stove; would not believe it could be beat, but I can do double the work with yours on the same cost, and the heat is better distributed."

A. Coulter & Co., Watches and Jewelry, 46 Jackson Street: "We never had our large office and salesroom so comfortable *all over*, and *one* heater does it. We also use your furnace in our residences."

S. E. Trefy: "I've handled a good many stoves in my time, but yours goes ahead of all of them."

☞We are in receipt of hundreds of letters giving good words for the Hess system of heating and ventilation.

THE BEST IS THE CHEAPEST.